THESE MODERN WOMEN

THESE MODERN WOMEN

AUTOBIOGRAPHICAL ESSAYS
FROM THE TWENTIES

EDITED AND WITH A REVISED INTRODUCTION BY
ELAINE SHOWALTER

THE FEMINIST PRESS
at The City University of New York
New York

Published 1989 by The Feminist Press at The City University of New York,
311 East 94 Street, New York, N.Y. 10128
Distributed by The Talman Company, Inc., 150 Fifth Avenue, New York, N.Y.
10011
Printed in the United States of America

93   92   91   90   89   5   4   3   2   1

This collection of essays was originally published in book form in 1979 by The
Feminist Press. This edition of *These Modern Women* contains a revised
introduction.

Library of Congress Cataloging-in-Publication Data

These modern women.

    Includes bibliographical references.

    1. Feminists—United States—Biography. 2. Women—Psychology.
3. United States—Social conditions—1918-1932. I. Showalter, Elaine.
HQ1412.T45   1989   305.4′2′0922   89-1153
ISBN 1-55861-007-3

This publication is made possible, in part, by public funds from the New York
State Council on the Arts.

Cover design by Paula Martinac
Photographs (from top to bottom): Inez Haynes Irwin; Genevieve Taggard;
Crystal Eastman; Ruth Pickering. The Feminist Press gratefully acknowledges
the Schlesinger Library on the History of Women in America, Radcliffe College,
for permission to reproduce these photographs on the cover of this book.

*To Violet Cottler
and Jean Showalter*

ACKNOWLEDGMENTS

I have had a great deal of help on this project from scholars and friends who have contributed their time and expertise. My husband, English Showalter, spent many hours tracking down "modern women" in library archives. Mari Jo Buhle researched Sue Shelton White, Cornelia Pinchot, Lorine Pruette, and Phyllis Blanchard, and I have made extensive use of her notes and comments. She and Ellen DuBois of the Feminist Press Reprints Committee read the introduction and offered many helpful suggestions. Lois Banner, William O'Neill, William Chafe, and Dorothy Ross helped a literary scholar find her way among historical sources. James P. Louis and Sanford S. Smoller provided information on Sue White and Victoria McAlmon; Grace Marrissael kindly let me use photographs and clippings from the McAlmon family collection. Lorine Pruette supplied information about her marriage and career; Blanche Wiesen Cook contributed information on Crystal Eastman. James J. Storrow of *The Nation* identified the women contributors, and he, Blair Clark, and Harry Maurer of *The Nation* encouraged and supported the project. As always, the staff of the Schlesinger Library at Radcliffe College was hospitable, patient, and knowledgeable, especially Candice Kalisher. Liz Phillips of The Feminist Press has been the "modern woman's" ideal editor. Special acknowledgments to Joan Kelly for her kind assistance.

TABLE OF CONTENTS

INTRODUCTION
by Elaine Showalter

Mary Austin was a "fighting feminist" who had been raised in a household where abolition, temperance, and women's suffrage were holy causes. Inez Haynes Irwin was "a firm believer in militant tactics," whose heart rejoiced at the first brick thrown by the English suffragettes. Genevieve Taggard was "a poet, a wine-bibber, a radical; a non-churchgoer who will no longer sing in the choir or lead prayer-meeting with a testimonial." Cornelia Bryce Pinchot enjoyed adventure and sought the stimulation and release of danger and even physical pain: "the stalling of an airplane engine low over London, picketing surrounded by a school of angry scabs, swimming among sharks."

These exuberant women were among the seventeen who were invited by the liberal magazine *The Nation*, in 1926 and 1927, to explore the personal sources of their feminism, and to show how their feminist ideals had stood up to the realities and pressures of the female life cycle. "Our object," the editors announced with the first installment of "These Modern Women" on December 1, 1926, "is to discover the origin of their modern point of view toward men, marriage, children, and jobs. Do spirited ancestors explain their rebellion? Or is it due to thwarted ambition or distaste for domestic drudgery?" Anonymity was offered as an encouragement to uninhibited self-disclosure and as protection against the hurt feelings of relatives or the abuse of strangers. When the series was completed, three well-known psychologists were asked to analyze, according to their specialties, why these women had chosen to live their lives as they did, and to speculate on what women might become.

The seventeen essays and three responses by psychologists are reprinted in this volume. The writings are of interest both for the light they shed on the era of the twenties and for the ways in which they illuminate the feminism of today.

What did it mean to be a "modern woman" in the 1920s? The answer did not lie in youth or the new generation; the median age of the *Nation* group was forty, and the women ranged from Mary Austin, who was fifty-eight and had heard Susan B. Anthony, to Lorine Pruette, who was thirty and a spirited participant in the psychoanalytic debates of the decade. Neither was modernism simply a question of politics or style. The *Nation* women included all the possibilities of 1920s feminism, both in terms of practical allegiances within the women's movement itself, and within the broader framework of feminist ideology. At one extreme were women like Sue Shelton White and Cornelia Bryce Pinchot, public feminists who were committed to women's issues, but almost single-mindedly from a legalistic, political, or civic perspective. Both made careers for themselves in politics—Pinchot as the campaigning wife of the successful politician Gifford Pinchot and as a member of the Council of Republican Women; White as the southern leader of the National Women's Party and a sturdy Democrat who worked for the National Recovery Administration (NRA) and the Social Security agency. For these powerful women who prided themselves on their ability to function brilliantly in a man's world, feminism meant the ability to break out of the restrictions binding women to limited aspirations or familial roles and to take on the challenges and responsibilities of public life.

At another extreme were radicals like Genevieve Taggard, Victoria McAlmon, and Crystal Eastman, socialists who connected feminism to class and race struggle and who envisioned revolutionary, not just legislative, redefinitions of the economic system, cultural values, and sex roles. Eastman had been one of the leaders, with Alice Paul, of the militant suffrage wing of the feminist movement. In the 1920s, Eastman was one of the most articulate and determined advocates of the National Women's Party and the Equal Rights Amendment, which she defended in a letter to *The Nation* in 1924:

The battle for "equal rights"....must be fought and it will be fought by a free-handed, non-partisan minority of energetic feminists to whom politics in general, even "reform" politics, will continue to be a matter of indifference so long as women are classed with children and minors in industrial legislation, so long as even in our most advanced States a woman can be penalized by the loss of her job when she marries. [1]

THE NEW-STYLE FEMINIST

The difference between the modern woman, and the suffragist or feminist of the nineteenth century, was her insistence on the right to self-fulfillment in both public life and in relationships with men. Where earlier feminist generations had renounced marriage in order to dedicate themselves to careers, the "truly modern" women, according to Dorothy Bromley's 1927 article, "Feminist—New Style," admitted "that a full life calls for marriage and children as well as a career." [2] To be modern meant to want heterosexual love as well as work; neither was sufficient by itself. However, the modern woman was not unaware of the difficulty in combining these goals.

As a group, the *Nation* women's most striking characteristic is their articulation of the dilemma of balancing marriage and career.

4

The modern woman, explained Crystal Eastman, is

not altogether satisfied with love, marriage, and a purely domestic career. She wants money of her own. She wants work of her own. She wants some means of self-expression, perhaps, some way of satisfying her personal ambitions. But she wants a husband, home and children, too. How to reconcile these two desires in real life, that is the question. [3]

Twelve of the seventeen *Nation* women—seventy percent—were, or had been, married in 1926. Three of the women had been divorced, a sign of their feminist insistence on satisfaction within the marital relationship. Three of the group, Sue White, Victoria McAlmon, and Kate Gregg, stayed single all their lives. It is important to understand how significantly this high percentage of married women differentiates the *Nation* group from a comparable group of feminists twenty-five years earlier. Nineteenth-century feminists did not see marriage and public life in conflict for women; they recognized them as mutually *exclusive*, and accepted the necessity of choosing between them. The *Nation* feminists expected to have both; and their disappointed expectations are the basis of contemporary feminism, which aims not for a "free" choice, but for life in both dimensions.

The modern woman was also different from her nineteenth-century counterpart in her reliance on the new science of psychology. Lorine Pruette and Phyllis Blanchard were both Ph.D.s who had studied with the eminent psychologist G. Stanley Hall at Clark University. They tried to solve women's dilemma, to integrate women's new access to economic and public life with private and personal fulfillment, through the newly popular methods of Freudian psychology and social science. In *New Girls for Old* (1930), Blanchard explained that even professional achievement was an inadequate recompense for the self-mutilation of celibacy and lovelessness: "The modern girl, who has seen the loneliness of older unmarried friends, is beginning to discount the rewards from a material success that must be accomplished at the expense of love." [4] The healthy psyche, balancing the needs for love and for achievement, was the goal of "modern" feminism; and psychology, as the *Nation* series shows in its structure and emphases, became the favored "modern" science for understanding women and society.

AN AVANT-GARDE

The *Nation* series was the brainchild of the young managing editor, Freda Kirchwey (1894-1976), herself a modern woman who chose contributors reflecting her own liberal politics and urban style. The daughter of George W. Kirchwey, dean of Columbia Law School and a former warden of Sing-Sing Prison, Freda Kirchwey "typified the upper-middle-class emancipated woman of this century."[5] As early as high school, she had become involved in suffrage activities, and at Barnard College, she led the movement to abolish sororities and picketed for striking New York garment workers. When she graduated in 1915, her classmates voted her "best looking, the one who has done the most for Barnard, most popular, most militant and the one most likely to be famous in the future." At twenty-four, she joined the staff of *The Nation*, and her socialist interests, her energy, and her intelligence brought her rapid success. She became managing editor in 1922, and fifteen years later she bought the magazine and ran it as editor and publisher until her retirement in 1955. In her private life, Kirchwey was a role model for the new life-style of career and marriage. When she married Evans Clark in 1916, she kept her own name; when she became pregnant, she continued to work right up to the birth date, and she returned to the office shortly after her son Michael was born.

During the 1920s, Kirchwey's influence on *The Nation* could be seen particularly in its support of women's issues. In 1924, she edited a symposium on "Our Changing Morality" which included a number of essays on female sexuality and its fulfillment. Defining herself politically as a "left-wing feminist and internationalist,"[6] Kirchwey rejected membership in Alice Paul's National Women's Party and sought to expand the concerns of the women's movement to include birth control, conditions of working women, the family, and world peace. She editorially opposed the Equal Rights Amendment and supported the trade union women who feared the loss of protective legislation.

Like Freda Kirchwey, the women who were asked to contribute to the series were "successful" women, prominent and economically mobile by virtue of their own activities, rather than through their fathers and husbands. Middle class, highly educated, and white, they were obviously an elite group. Yet they were representative of the transformation taking place in the lives of American women. The married middle-class woman, Mary Ross argued in *Woman's Coming of Age* (1931), is the best barometer of social change, because she is "not so protected by wealth and social position as to ignore changes in social pressures, yet...has sufficient leeway beyond the requirements of mere existence to admit of change and occasional experimentation."[7] As professional women, they were also placed in a situation of more acute sensitivity to role conflict than women who lived entirely within the female culture.

As working professionals, the *Nation* contributors represented a small minority of American women—about fourteen percent of a female labor force which included less than a quarter of all women between the ages of twenty and sixty-four. Starting out in small towns all over the country (eight were from New England, four from the South, four from the Middle West, and one from the Far West), they had gravitated to the cities, especially to New York. Lorine Pruette and Phyllis Blanchard had taught at Columbia; Genevieve Taggard, Mary Austin, and Crystal Eastman were frequent contributors to the New York radical press; Elizabeth Stuyvesant had worked for the Socialist party in the mayoralty election of 1917; Inez Irwin, Mary Hopkins, and Alice Kimball successfully entered the popular journalism market; Lou Rogers sold political cartoons to the New York *Call*; and Wanda Gág had her first one-woman show at New York's Weyhe Gallery in 1926. Four of the women had Ph.D.s; two were lawyers.

Many of the *Nation* women emphasized their privileged status by membership in Heterodoxy, a New York feminist society organized in 1912 by the Unitarian minister Marie Jenny Howe. Virtually every prominent suffragist, activist, and woman professional in New York, including Agnes de Mille, Elizabeth Gurley Flynn, Zona Gale, and Charlotte Perkins Gilman, attended the biweekly Saturday lunch meetings of Heterodoxy, to hear talks in which, according to Inez Irwin, "a member told whatever she chose to reveal about her girlhood, childhood, young womanhood." The atmosphere of these meetings was intensely feminist and emotional.[8] In their informal structure, their process of personal sharing, and their emphasis on mutual support, the meetings of Heterodoxy resembled the consciousness-raising sessions of the women's liberation movement of the 1960s and 1970s. The interest in family background in the *Nation* essays owes something to Heterodoxy, as well as to the tradition of autobiography in American feminism and to the new popularity of psychology.

If their professional careers set these modern women apart from the majority of their contemporaries, so did their childbearing status. Although the *Nation* women generally did not choose between marriage and career, and placed great emphasis on having both, most of them rejected motherhood; only five of the women had children. This figure reflects both the unpopularity of motherhood among career women early in the century and the strong reaction against female cul-

7

ture of this particular group. Many came from large families (Inez Irwin was one of seventeen children) and had seen their mothers worn out with constant childbearing. Irwin felt "a profound horror of the woman's life," and set out to separate herself from female culture by rejecting all of its skills; she vowed never to learn how to sew, knit, or cook. Lorine Pruette's mother, forced by her physician to endure childbirth without chloroform because the Bible said women should suffer, filled her daughter with wrath against the injustice of a world in which "women had all the children and men had all the fun." Kate Gregg witnessed her mother, pregnant with her sixth child, putting a loaded revolver under her pillow; she planned to kill herself if she went into labor when her husband was off on one of his frequent alcoholic binges. Other of the women, like Wanda Gág, wanted children badly but finally decided that they would not be able to combine their careers with motherhood.

The 1920s emphasis on psychology, personal fulfillment, and the problems of the individual psyche often obscures the problems and obstacles women were still facing collectively in their relation to the American economy: the resistance of the male-dominated professional guilds to accept women and the low rate of female participation in the labor movement; the continuing segregation of women workers into low-status job categories; the disparity between the pay of men and women; and the increasing devaluation of domestic work. While the number of women employed increased during the decade, women collectively did not make significant economic gains. Three out of four professional women went into teaching, nursing, and other traditional women's fields. The number of women doctors declined; of 482 general hospitals, only 40 accepted women interns. The prestigious law schools refused to accept women; the percentage of women lawyers did not increase between 1920 and 1930. Women received one out of every seven Ph.D.s awarded, but were only 4 percent of the full professors in universities. By 1924, only 2.94 percent of working women were unionized.[9]

Thus in their "modernity," their mobility, their choice of careers, and their control of their bodies, the *Nation* women were an avant-garde, different from the housewife of Middletown who still lived in a sexually segregated world, and also different from the urban and rural women who worked hard all their lives because they needed the money. Indeed, there were complaints that these women were hardly typical.

One reader from Brooklyn wrote indignantly to *The Nation* to present the case of the woman factory worker:

Sir: We were packing chocolate-covered cherries on the night shift in a candy factory. We pack from the belt conveyor which carries the candy from the dipping machine through the cooler, and our hands move fast, but we talk. The younger woman wants to know what she is missing by not being married. She makes the older woman answer thus:

"Sure I'm married; do I look like a chicken? Me oldest girl is sixteen. I got six kids. Work hard? My God, with six kids, watchu think? Yestday I washed eight lines clothes meself. Today I iron them. I work all the time by night in factory. Last week I worked in hemp factory. I give it up, too hard. Me girl she earn good money in factory; but she's girl, she need money herself. Me husband and me we always fight now. I have always to keep still and give in. It looks not nice for the children. I say, 'Yeh, yeh, you right,' and he keep still too. We fight about the children. He wants I should be strict and teach them bedder. I got no time; I should worry what he say. I'm tired of me husband. Sixteen years long time to live with man. Get tired of dress, house, friend, everything, husband too.

"But I'm not crazy. I got six kids. They need father. They need eat. Anyway, who know what devil I get if I leave me husband? I know what I got." And, turning to the younger woman: "You better get married anyway. Married is bad enough, but single is worse."

There is one of These Modern Women for you—an ultra-modern woman, product of our up-to-date industrial system: mother of six, housekeeper for eight, wageworker, all in one.

FEMINISM'S AWKWARD AGE

The *Nation* series is especially poignant because it appeared at the point when suffragists, activists, and radicals were having to acknowledge the awkward reality of a declining American feminism. In recent years, historians studying various aspects of social and radical feminism in the postsuffrage years agree that 1925 is the turning point, both in terms of legislative success and the morale of individual women.[10] The collapse of the suffrage coalition, the factionalization of the women's movement into bitterly opposed parties, and the absence of a clearly defined female voting bloc contributed to the political decline. On the personal level, the difficulty of applying feminist theory to daily life in a society still organized on patriarchal principles, and the younger generation's disavowal of the ideals and goals of the women's movement, led to fatigue and withdrawal among former leaders. At the end of the decade, Phyllis Blanchard described a pervasive sense of disillusion: "In a sense, we may say that women have been asking impossible values from work, from love, from politics, and from religion. But none have permanently served, at least so far as the majority of the sex is concerned."[11]

The essays both illustrate this phenomenon and give us a new perspective on it. These women thought that there were no more major structural changes to be fought for that would affect all women. The Nineteenth Amendment was the crowning collective victory. From now on, progress, or lack of it, was to be measured in individual terms, not in the situation of the whole sex. Feminists of the twenties had not changed their minds about the attractions of a life combining work, marriage, and motherhood. They had simply discovered that such a life was still unattainable, and they interpreted their inability to find exciting jobs and reliable child care as personal failures, rather than challenging the patriarchal assumptions of American society. One of the strongest themes of the essays is the equation of disillusion and maturity. "Growing up" is defined as the loss of faith in collectivism and rebellion. "I no longer work on movements," writes Alice Kimball. Mary Alden Hopkins substitutes an individualistic pragmatism for her earlier principled protest. Lorine Pruette, calling her essay "The Evolution of Disenchantment," writes that at the age of thirty-one she had "lost all my motivating faiths, faith in the righteous cause of women, faith in the recreating powers of science, faith in the ennobling possibilities of education." Instead, she thought of a Utopia without principles, full of strong individuals seeking self-gratification with "magnificent and flaming audacity." In the essays we can see these attitudes as responses to careers moving more slowly than the women had hoped, to difficult personal lives, to rejection in politics and in the higher levels of the professions, to the daily slog of earning one's living in a man's world. Some of the women, notably Crystal Eastman and Cornelia Pinchot, had never wavered in their feminist faith. But as a group the *Nation* women present a clear picture of adjustment, whether resigned or defiant, to a struggle without glamour or recognition waged by each woman alone in her home or office.

The feminist crash of the twenties came as a painful shock, so painful that it took history several decades to face up to it. A few old-guard suffrage leaders had anticipated the dangerous aftereffects of the end of the campaign. "I am sorry for you young women who have to carry on the work in the next ten years, for suffrage was a symbol, and you have lost your symbol," Anna Howard Shaw told Emily Blair. "There is nothing for women to rally around."[12] Most suffragists had predicted that an enfranchised female electorate would vote for sweeping social reforms, bring an end to war, and eliminate drug traffic, prostitution, and venereal disease. Like the temperance forces with whom they had forged strong political alliances, many suffragists had devoted their lives to the passage of a constitutional amendment. They had an enormous psychological investment in its successful transformation of American society. For them to admit, only a few years after the struggle, that they had been mistaken was to concede the fallacy of their most fundamental feminist assumptions about the spiritual superiority of women. On the other side, those who had opposed the extension of freedom represented by women's suffrage wanted to deny the need for any further emancipation. Thus it was in their interest as well to applaud the era of the "new woman," to cede defeat gracefully and welcome the age of freedom, knowing all the while that giving women the vote had altered few basic patterns of American society and threatened few male enclaves. As Edward S. Martin genially observed in 1926, "Nevertheless, women suffrage is a good thing if only to have it over."[13]

The hard political evidence of the insufficiency of the suffrage amendment was apparent very early in the decade. When women fought for suffrage, they fought together, united and sustained by a single goal and by each other's sisterly support. But when women went to vote, they went alone. And as voters their record was unimpressive—both in terms of turnout at the polls and cohesion on issues. Historians explain this substantially in terms of the pressures newly enfranchised women faced from male opposition in their families, and the tendency of all new voters to follow the lead of family authorities or to abstain.

Moreover, party politics were tedious and mundane after the heightened rhetoric, the sisterhood, and the sense of history created by the suffragists. As early as 1921, Carrie Chapman Catt noted the feeling of anticlimax:

Suffrage women last autumn numerously confessed that they found real politics "pale and insipid" when it came time to use their first vote. It seemed sordid and commonplace to be striving merely to elect men whose platforms were so strangely confused they could not find a direct issue. They felt a vacancy where for years there had been purpose consecrated to an immortal principle.[14]

At the party conventions, the women's sense of exclusion from party traditions, from policy decisions, and from the informal but impenetrable networks of the male culture was typically translated into the ancient and consoling stereotype that politics was the activity of overgrown boys. Reporting on the Democratic convention of 1924 for *The Nation*, Ernestine Evans wondered, "Did I spend seven years fighting for suffrage and earn the right to be part of a convention that wastes days over an issue of whether men shall parade the street in nightshirts and astonish with fireworks, Judas and the Pope, and 'Old Black Joe'?"[15]

In anticipation of the "woman's vote," the political parties, Congress, and officeholders had initially moved to conciliate and win female support by passing social reform legislation, especially that dealing with maternity and infancy. The Sheppard-Towner Bill of 1921 appropriated funds for instruction on maternal and infant health, and the Child Labor Amendment was passed in 1924. But male politicians quickly realized that their positions were secure, that they had nothing to fear from women as an organized bloc of voters. Reckoned in terms of the power to seize or control leadership of key committees and districts, women were a negligible force. Even a Democratic committeewoman, Emily Newell Blair, admitted that women in organized politics could not count on sexual solidarity as a bargaining tool: "I know of no woman today who has any influence or political power because she is a woman. I know of no woman who has a following of other women. I know of no politician who is afraid of the woman vote on any question under the sun."[16] Measured by this scale, women's suffrage could be described as a failure. "Is Women's Suffrage a Failure?" asked Charles E. Russell in 1924; in 1925, Emily Blair asked "Are Women A Failure in Politics?" By 1925, according to historian William Chafe, "Women's standing in the eyes of politicians dropped precipitously. . . .Congressmen seemed as intent on rebuffing the requests of female reformers in the second half of the decade as they had been in granting them during the first half."[17]

On the personal and psychological level, the sense of failure was even more dispiriting and acute. Feminism had stopped being controversial and had become irrelevant, or so it seemed to observers of the young women of the 1920s. In 1927, Lorine Pruette wrote that American women under fifty fell into three groups. In the first group were "those who struggled for independence of action, who have against legal and social disqualifications fought their way into positions of importance, who bore the brunt of the fight begun in their day and who never quite lose their bitterness toward men." Pruette's second group was "a younger group which knows less bitterness because it has known less of the struggle." The third group Pruette described was "a still younger group that is frankly amazed at all the feminist pother and likely to be bored when the subject comes up."[18] In her research, Pruette investigated the aspirations and expectations of teenage girls, documenting the failure of the suffragists to change the basic patterns of sex-role conditioning. In *Women and Leisure* (1924), Pruette published the discouraging evidence that middle-class teenage girls in New York and Tennessee did not want careers; the few who wanted to work had vague Hollywood fantasies of glamorous jobs. Their heroines were Joan of Arc and Cleopatra, romantic figures of the past rather than realistic modern role models. In another shift, graduates of the top women's colleges in the 1920s expressed a preference for marriage over a career. A poll of Vassar women in 1923 showed ninety percent wishing marriage, and only eleven percent planning careers.[19]

Egged on by advertising, which doubled in volume during the 1920s, and by the fashion and cosmetics industries, women, by the end of the decade, began to praise the old-fashioned "privileges" of femininity and the joys of "spending the day in strictly feminine pursuits." Feminists deplored these fantasies of dependent domesticity as pernicious and self-destructive. What privilege amounted to, wrote Alice Beal Parsons, was "getting everything out of some man that one can." In trying to hold on to the special perquisites of dependent and submissive femininity, Parsons realized, women could never aspire to equality. "When these daughters of the generation that achieved independence get back their privileges," she predicted, "they will find that they have lost their rights."[20] Lorine Pruette and the radical feminist Suzanne LaFollette were especially concerned with the intellectual casualties of the Feminine Mystique. In *Concerning Women* (1926) LaFollette argued that American consumerism, technology, and capitalism combined to stupefy the most profound human impulses, and that women, hypnotized by advertising, leisure, and luxuries, lived "without the exercise of the reflective intellect, without ideas, without ideals, and in a proper use of the word without emotions."[21] Pruette worried about the inevitable mental deterioration caused by "many years of uninterrupted domesticity,"[22] anticipating the concern of contemporary feminists that women's self-esteem and energy declines through forced isolation in the family and continued immersion in the unchallenging monotony of domestic routine.

TRYING TO BE MODERN:
IDENTIFYING WITH MEN

Feminists in the 1920s often saw their problems as the inevitable turmoil of transition. Women, they explained, were seeking new roles and therefore were confused and vulnerable. "Out in the world, in contact and competition with men," wrote Freda Kirchwey, "[woman] is forced to discriminate: questions are thrust upon her. The old rules fail to work; bewildering inconsistencies confront her...slowly, clumsily, she is trying to construct a way out to a new sort of certainty in life...."[23] Lorine Pruette pointed out that the modern woman was unsure of herself, and thus easily manipulated or defeated: "Nothing is settled in the woman's mind. She is having to work out new ways of living, about which there are still many disputes. She has not the ready-made justifications of the men."[24] Women's conflicts and uncertainties were the result of their experience of continuing discrimination in the job market and continuing responsibility for the quality of domestic life. They were seeking a life-style for which there were few precedents and even fewer social and political supports.

A major source of conflict was the transformation in American sexual mores and attitudes towards female sexuality. In the nineteenth century, women were allowed and even encouraged to form close emotional relationships with other women, intimate friendships that spanned their lives. Heterosexual friendships, however, were restricted, and many women grew to maturity with a strong internalized aversion to physical sexuality.[25] This inhibition could become a source of spiritual and political power. Liberation for nineteenth-century feminists included "the right to abstain from sexual relations,"[26] and women's supposed lack of sexual appetite was a source of their spiritual superiority. Furthermore, a strong motivation to avoid marriage vastly simplified the career decisions and the apportionment of energies in women's lives. But the twentieth century redefined female sexuality, cutting short the "homosocial ties of girlhood," and impelling "the emerging woman of thirteen or fourteen toward heterosexual relationships."[27]

In July 1927, the oldest woman in the *Nation* group, Mary Austin, examined some of the changes. Born in 1868, Austin recalled how

In those late nineteenth-century decades all the disabilities of excessive child-bearing were charged to the horrid appetites of the husband. Not only did the current phrases of birth control and contraceptives not come into use until the women of the pioneer suffrage generations were past being interested in them, but nobody, positively *nobody*, had yet suggested that women are passionately endowed even as men are; not good women! That sexual desire was something to which God in his inscrutable wisdom had sacrificed all women, was so certainly believed by my mother's generation that it was never even successfully camouflaged by preachers and teachers with blague about the sanctity of motherhood. But my own generation still lacked even a vocabulary by which measures of escape could be intelligently discussed. As for the convenient and illuminating terminology of "sex psychology" with which modern youth mitigates its own confusion, everyone knows that it was still some twenty years ahead. [28]

It was because of this ignorance and inhibition, Austin thought, that women of her generation, who had grown up in the late nineteenth century, had felt so much sex-antagonism, and had believed "that the chief obstacle to all they most wished for was to be found in the maleness of men."

Unlike their mothers, however, the "modern" women struggled to overcome sex-antagonism, which they associated with prudery and provincialism. Pruette and Blanchard were exposed to Freudian psychoanalytic theory about the importance of sexuality in human experience, and painfully overcame the puritanism in their childhood conditioning to acknowledge their own sexual needs. Garland Smith, too, educated herself with Freud and Hall. Many of the other women had liberated attitudes toward sexuality and had had lovers. "Love is good wherever it comes from" wrote Lou Rogers. Elizabeth Stuyvesant, living unmarried and happy with the same man for eleven years, could imagine "room in my life for other close relationships." Crystal Eastman had planned to go to Italy and have an illegitimate child if she was not married by the age of twenty-nine; she made the deadline, however, with seventeen days to spare.

While the encounter with sexuality—with heterosexual experience—was essential to women's freedom, it also had negative and far-reaching effects on the structure of a women's movement. Three contemporary historians of feminism have explained that:

With the reaffirmation of feminine sexuality, the traditional notion of sisterhood broke down....Women in the twentieth century learned that they were supposed to have emotional attachments only to men. In this way, because women competed on an individual basis for men's attention, the possibilities for women coming together to develop feminist consciousness and realize their own power lessened. [29]

We see this change in many aspects of the essays, such as the absence of any discussion of female relationships, a remarkable hiatus in an American feminist tradition of strong female bonding; one thinks, for example, of the letters of Susan B. Anthony and Elizabeth Cady Stanton. For many of the *Nation* women, the role model seems to be the "Feminist—New Style," defined by Dorothy Bromley in 1927. The new-style feminist is a good dresser, a good sport, and a pal; she resembles the gallant heroines of Fitzgerald's short stories. She feels no need to defend or exaggerate the achievements or the capabilities of women collectively; she "freely admits that American women have so far achieved but little in the arts, sciences, and professions as compared with men." She does not identify with women and prefers to work with men, "for their methods are more direct, and their view larger, and she finds that she can deal with them on a basis of frank comradeship." Comradeship must lead eventually to marriage, for the new-style feminist believes that husband and children are necessary to the average woman's fullest development, and that free love is an impractical arrangement for the family. About the only redeeming feature of this new-style feminism, as Bromley defines it, is the insistence on a free exchange within marriage—and the commitment to be useful and productive in some way; as Bromley says, "to fit her abilities to some kind of work." But the work is conceded from the start to be inferior to the work of men. Having succeeded in her purposes, the new-style feminist congratulates herself that she has matured, and "expressed herself." In "A Deflated Rebel," Ruth Pickering gives a good description of this point of view: "I have traded my sense of exhilarating defiance (shall we call it feminism?) for an assurance of free and unimpeded self-expression (or shall we call that feminism?). In other words I have grown up."

In practice, "growing up" meant accepting second-class status gracefully and finding the most satisfactory personal compromise. The business world made no voluntary adjustments to women's needs; despite numerical increases, women were still denied top positions even in favorable fields. Explaining that men saw women as "a sort of innately secretarial sex," Elizabeth Kemper Adams warned aspiring professional women that:

They will have to learn not to ask or expect any concessions whatever on the grounds that they are women, nor even sometimes on the grounds that they are human, since any weakness is likely to be considered feminine. They will have to expect to be judged even more rigorously than young men of the same education doing similar work, and to breathe an atmosphere of being on trial. [30]

TRYING TO BE MODERN:
CAREER, MARRIAGE, AND MOTHERHOOD

In 1921, Adams found the relations of professional women to marriage and parenthood "a topic in too unsettled and transitional a state" for discussion. The random or part-time work, often clerical, of the new-style feminist, which brought in money, but did not require painful or disturbing reorganization of the sexual division of labor, was a kind of solution to the dilemma.

Even the highly motivated *Nation* women had erratic careers, and few had children. Despite their success relative to other women in the labor market, they were "at the bottom of the top" of their professions. The reputations of even the most distinguished among them have not survived their era, and a few have altogether disappeared from history, from guidebooks and yearbooks and directories. Only Wanda Gág and Genevieve Taggard had a strong sense of vocation as girls and deliberately set out to make themselves artists. Some of the women experimented with a variety of experiences and occupations before marriage or the establishment of a career. Others—Kate Gregg, Mary Hopkins, and Sue White—were held back by family obligations, sex discrimination, and financial problems, and did not enter their profession until their thirties. More than half of the *Nation* group were writers with various specialties, who worked at home and were able to arrange flexible schedules that did not conflict with their husbands' needs and demands, a solution open to very few women in the work force.

Either an independent single life—or childless marriages—and careers essentially independent of the office and the time clock enabled most of the *Nation* women to pursue their goals. The women who never married cite both ideological reservations and specific demands from prospective suitors. Sue Shelton White thought that "marriage is too much of a compromise; it lops off a woman's life as an individual. Yet the renunciation too is a lopping-off. We choose between the frying-pan and the fire—both very uncomfortable." Her rejected suitors, and those of Kate Gregg, another woman who remained single, envisioned domesticity, their would-be wives in homes with big kitchens. Other women were more fortunate in meeting men, as Wanda Gág writes, who not only were willing to put up with independent wives, "but actually seemed to prefer this attitude in women." Phyllis Blanchard, for whom the struggle between the need for love and the need for independence was central in her life, married at thirty, to a "man of insight, imagination, and humor, who cherishes no desire to be owner or tyrant. He respects my work as much as I do his." Lorine Pruette also found a supportive husband, with "few theories about woman's position, or man's."

Although Dorothy Bromley, Lorine Pruette, and Phyllis Blanchard were optimistic that career, marriage, and even family could be satisfactorily combined for the modern woman, the changes in the home and in domestic work required to support such a life-style did not take place during the 1920s. As early as 1903, Charlotte Perkins Gilman, in *The Home*, had advocated fundamental changes in the domestic patterns and customs of American life and had launched an attack on the nuclear family. In 1915, Henrietta Rodman, a leader of the radical Greenwich Village Feminist Alliance, had proposed a new kind of housing for professional women, incorporating many of Gilman's arguments and providing for the centralization of what Rodman called the "four primitive home industries"—child care, cooking, housework, and laundry. Plans were prepared by an architect for a model apartment building in Washington Square which would utilize the latest technology and include space for a communal kitchen and day nursery. Professional cooks and teachers, hired by the families in the apartment, were to take over the tasks of food preparation and child care, freeing the mothers for their careers. Rodman understood that child care would become the central issue in women's professional success:

At the present time the care of the baby is the weak point in feminism. The care of children, particularly those under four or five years of age, is the point at which feminism is most open to attack. We must have this apartment house before we can become honest feminists.[31]

But the apartment was never constructed. Another short-lived 1920s effort to work out ways for women to share and simplify home management was Ethel Puffer Howes' Institute for the Coordination of Women's Interests, at Smith College, which addressed itself to the concrete problem of finding a supportive environment to facilitate women's professional aspirations. The Institute ran cooperative nurseries and laundries, and seminars on efficient and thrifty food preparation.

Howes hoped "to prove that the wife and mother can so adjust her home problems that she can carry on a profession or a line of occupation."[32]

But even these radical programs perpetuated the assumption that women, whether they worked or not, must accept full responsibility for the home and for children. Recalling her "almost perfect" parents, both of whom were ministers and suffragists, Crystal Eastman described an experimental houskeeping collective organized by her mother with three other families in their summer community. Cleaning, meal planning, shopping, gardening, and paying tradesmen rotated among the families—but really only among the mothers. A cook prepared all meals. The fathers, as always, were free of household obligations. As family sociologist Ernest Groves observed, the changes in the role of the wife and mother had led to "no corresponding reconstruction of the role of husband."[33] Of course, husbands were not eager to have *their* roles reconstructed, as many modern women realized.[34] In "Fifty-Fifty Wives," Mary Alden Hopkins speculated on egalitarian marriages: "Housework is difficult to divide with a man, though there is nothing in the work itself to make this so. The trouble lies in the different attitudes which men and women have toward housework. The woman just naturally does the work and the man just naturally does not."[35] Lorine Pruette observed sardonically that upon marriage, "men appear to lose a large part of their capacity as adults: they can no longer feed themselves, house themselves, look after their health, or attend to their social responsibilities (most of them upon marriage lose the capacity even of writing to their own mother)."[36]

Only the most extreme feminists, such as Suzanne LaFollette and Alice Beal Parsons, dared suggest that men too might work part-time and share the responsibilities of child care—or even of running the home. "When she does as much work outside the home as her husband," wrote Parsons in *Woman's Dilemma*, "there would seem to be no reason why she should in the future be responsible for all the domestic chores."[37] Parsons argued for thorough modernization of the home, the family, and the workplace, in order to make it possible for women to lead full, free lives. Among her other suggestions were centralized catering kitchens, industrialized housecleaning, payment for mothers at home, day care for children, and flexible work hours. All of these could be achieved, she believed, without sacrificing the essential qualities of the home and family; indeed, they would preserve and support family life, and enable both parents to participate in it.

In reality, however, public policy and industry had made few adjustments to women's raised aspirations. Margaret Sanger's birth control clinic had opened in New York in 1916, and for middle-class women, contraceptive information and devices allowed a measure of control of their reproductive lives. But the alliance between the birth control movement and the women's movement failed to develop during the 1920s, so that its revolutionary potential declined.[38] The nursery school movement was in its infancy, and only a few schools provided lunch, so that children came home in the middle of the day. Working women had to hire other women to come to their homes and take care of their children. For wealthy women, of course, this had always been an accepted and convenient method of child rearing.[39] Freda Kirchwey had little difficulty finding someone to look after her son. In the 1930s she wrote:

It really hasn't been any problem. I've always been able to find good competent maids and good schools. I know how difficult it must be for women who live in smaller communities where expert help is hard to get and where there aren't such good schools. In New York, everything can be made so simple.[40]

But even in the privileged *Nation* group, the most enthusiastic mother was also the wealthiest: Cornelia Bryce Pinchot, who wrote of the "adventure of child-bearing" with idiosyncratic appreciation of the thrilling release of intense physical pain.

For every Kirchwey or Pinchot who "succeeded," thousands of women "failed" in the adventure of feminism. By 1926, "confessions of ex-feminists" began to appear in American magazines, consciously wry, self-deprecating accounts of dissipated energy, frustration, and lost ideals which thinly masked the women's disappointment and anger. Edith Clark's "Trying to Be Modern," for example, which *The Nation* published in 1927, told a truth which the exuberant crusaders had ignored. Prepared for a life of career and motherhood, Clark gave up her job to follow her husband to a small rural community where, ten years out of college, she found "no provision made for the non-domestic matron; no pre-school groups, no trained cooks or nursemaids, and very few jobs." Housework, which she had expected to be mechanical, industrialized, and simple, "was to me desperately hard work." Pregnancy, which she had learned was a comfortable natural process that would not inconvenience her in any way, turned out to be a much more complicated business. And yet, it is important to note, Clark persisted, selling free-lance articles like the one *The Nation* published. The spate of articles by "ex-feminists" suggests that women were exploiting a journalistic market eager for such confessions, and, perhaps also, that those who went home were seeking opportunities to defend themselves. Actually, most ex-feminists, like Edith Clark, were modifying their original blueprints, rather than destroying them entirely.[41] Ruth Pickering, who describes herself as a "deflated rebel," stayed active as a journalist for twenty-five years.

Still, the issues of competition, role conflict, and compromise which the modern women described were real. In a bitter, eloquent, and remarkably modern article published in 1931, Lorine Pruette explained, "Why Women Fail." Like contemporary feminist sociologists, Pruette saw women as conditioned to lead lives as vicarious achievers, channeling their own needs and aggressions through others. Until women could cease to live contingent lives, in every respect, they could never compete successfully with men or find their own strength and joy. Women failed because they were under less economic pressure to succeed, because they were used to working for and through other people, because they wished to please, and, finally, because their husbands did not wish them to succeed. Witty, even comic in tone, Pruette's essay is nonetheless deeply pessimistic about women's opportunities. "The woman who wishes to be famous," she concludes, "should not marry; rather, she should attach to herself one or more women who will fetch and carry for her in the immemorial style of 'wives'; women who will secure her from interruption, give her freedom from the irritating small details of living, assure her that she is great, and devote their lives to making her so."[42]

EXPLAINING WOMEN: THEN

The three psychologists chosen by *The Nation* to explain modern women were all known in their fields and represented three important schools of 1920s thought on human behavior. The very idea of bringing in expert psychologists to comment on and analyze cultural and personal events is typical of the twenties fascination with human motivation, and especially with Freudian psychoanalysis; their views will seem very familiar to women of today.

The most optimistic of the three was the woman, Beatrice M. Hinkle, a physician who had become a Jungian psychoanalyst, and a feminist who attended meetings of Hererodoxy. In 1924, Hinkle wrote an article on "Women and the New Morality" for *The Nation*, in which she defended women's assertion of their sexuality as the triumph of reality over a repressive cultural ideal. Hinkle saw modern women as normal and natural, seeking through their feminist activities ways to develop and expand. The individualism of the women struck her too; she comments that their feminism was based, not on principle, but on "the necessities of their personal life." With all her sympathy, Hinkle nonetheless finds the women unfulfilled and "weak on the side of their woman's nature." As a group, she writes, "the general deduction to be drawn is that the love life is meager and that little enrichment of the personalities through the love experience has been gained." But she saw the women as transitional figures on the way to a new integration of all human capacities, literally mothers of a new race.

The two male psychologists were much more critical of the women, much more didactic about female sexual health, and much more pessimistic about the future of feminism. John B. Watson, who belligerently titled his piece "The Weakness of Women," was the 1920s guru of behaviorist psychology.[43] In 1919, Watson had been asked to resign his professorship at Johns Hopkins University because his espousal of behaviorist theory had become so fanatical and monolithic. He then became the vice-president of a prominent advertising agency, and his articles and books in the 1920s boosted behaviorism as the *only* valid psychology and the answer to all human dilemmas. Watson believed that people were machines programmed to function only by stimuli in their environment. Freudianism, which looked to infancy and early childhood for the psychic sources of behavior and feeling, was "voodoo" to Watson; he dismissed heredity and instinct, the basic categories of classic psychology, as well. Watson's manual of child rearing, advocating rigid maternal control of the child's environment and a rational approach to emotional displays, became the handbook of millions of American mothers virtually up to the era of Dr. Spock.

In many respects, behaviorist theory was antithetical to feminist values. The ideal end product of behaviorist control was a self-disciplined, highly productive, hard-working male cultural ideal. The extraordinary popularity of behaviorism in the 1920s was closely related to its promise of creating a population of go-getting, hard-nosed businessmen. Emotions were counterproductive elements in human engineering, and Watson enthusiastically heralded the coming age of reason:

The time will come when it will be just as bad manners in the home to be afraid, to sulk, to be over-emotional, seclusive, whiny, to show affection to mother, father, or other members of the family, as to come to the table with unwashed hands. [44]

On the other hand, behaviorism was an egalitarian psychology, which insisted that all human beings, white, black, rich, poor, male, and female, had equally innate capacities. By changing the environment, constantly reinforcing the desired traits and discouraging the undesirable ones, society could produce the kind of citizens it wished. Translated into the terms of sex-role conditioning, this theory has affinities with some current feminist theory. But Watson never made the obvious connections between social systems and social conditioning, never seemed quite to realize that people were already being programmed to fit social needs. In his analysis of the *Nation* women, he declared that "the great weakness of women [who seek careers] is that they have never been trained to work like men." If only mothers would teach their girls from infancy "habits of manipulation, skilful technique, endurance," they too would have successful careers. What Watson misses altogether is the collective large-scale resistance to women's work which made such individual solutions impossible. He denies that there had been "any insuperable difficulties which kept women from succeeding," and yet in the next paragraph he insists that "the having of children is almost an insuperable barrier to a career." His own fear and rejection of militant women is strongly voiced, and he accuses them of not having made a "sex adjustment." In short, Watson gives out conflicting messages to women, and in the end he blames women for being too "weak" to compete, rather than suggesting ways in which society might facilitate and reinforce women's strength. The behaviorist views of Lorine Pruette and Phyllis Blanchard, on the other hand, were modified by their understanding that women had been taught attitudes and behaviors that made life convenient and comfortable for men. No amount of personal and individual growth and change on women's part could succeed without a corresponding adjustment in social structure and sex roles generally.

Joseph Collins, a prominent neurologist who had made a name for himself as a popularizer of medical psychology (in books like *The Doctor Looks at Love and Life*), shared Watson's contempt for Freud, whom he linked with Christian Science, transcendentalism, and other "bosh, rot and nonsense." [45] Apart from their hearty rejection of

23

Freud, the two doctors had widely divergent views of human psychology, yet they reacted to the modern woman with similar distress. Of the three psychologists, Collins was the most conservative, and his views on the proper functions of women and men were nicely adjusted to allow men to do as they pleased and prevent women from doing much of anything. Collins cited God's will as his authority. Men were responsible for replenishing and subduing the earth, under which category Collins included every activity from flying the Atlantic nonstop to scientific research. Women were responsible for being fruitful and multiplying, and Collins thought that they should multiply five to ten times each. The unfruitful *Nation* group struck him as woefully low in their "sex-coefficient" and probably emotionally disturbed. At the end of his essay, he judges the romantic and sexual potential of the essayists and chooses the most and least appealing and fantasies himself as their lovers. Lorine Pruette and Lou Rogers were his favorites, and Mary Alden Hopkins and Alice Mary Kimball frightened him the most.

Obviously, the women could not respond to the psychologists without violating their anonymity, but Floyd Dell, an ardent former Greenwich Village radical and feminist, wrote to protest. In "Explaining (Some) Men," Dell pointed out the complacent sexism in the pieces by both Watson and Collins, especially their emphasis on the sexuality of the women. "It is remarkable to have Behaviorism and Neurology in such perfect agreement, not only with each other, but with the poolroom (that last male refuge, now that the polling-place and barbershop have been invaded). And now you know your places, girls. Back to the bedroom!"

All the psychologists, even Beatrice Hinkle, focus on the women's private lives and on the absence of details about love and marriage in their narratives. All of them assume that women who do not define themselves through their relationships with men have no love in their lives, and are, as Hinkle wrote, "weak on the side of their woman's nature." In fact, most of the women enjoyed enriching, varied, and successful relationships with men. It is also worth pointing out that despite the stresses of their new professional roles and their struggles with their personal lives, these modern women were stable, strong, and at peace with themselves. Throughout their life histories, there is no alcoholism, no mental breakdown, no suicide—in short, none of the diseases of modern womanhood which are so essential to fiction. Real women, as we have always known, are much more resilient and resourceful than our fictional heroines have been.

MODERN WOMEN: THEN AND NOW

The parallels between American women in the 1920s and the 1980s are striking and instructive. Half a century after the National Women's Party first proposed it, the Equal Rights Amendment suffered a seemingly irreversible defeat in June 1982, when the ratification deadline passed. As in the 1920s, the media are once again proclaiming the "Post-Feminist Generation," announcing that "ordinary" women are disenchanted with feminism.[46] Popular magazines repeatedly publish stories about dynamic, ambitious, professional women who "make it to the top" only to find they really want to be traditional wives and mothers after all. The "new traditionalist," advertisers tell us once again, is the woman who stays home to enjoy the privileges of being feminine. In the wake of the 1988 election, there is debate about whether the "gender gap" in voting patterns exists at all, or whether the women's vote can be discounted. Many of the hard-earned gains of the 1970s, such as legalized abortion and affirmative action programs, are under systematic and serious attack. It is easy for contemporary feminists, like some of the modern women of the 1920s, to feel discouraged, deflated, and disillusioned by what seems to be the reversal of the triumphs of the women's movement.

Yet fundamental changes have taken place in the lives of American women over the past decades as well, and these transformations of the labor force, marriage, and family cannot be easily reversed. By 1986, women's participation in the labor force had grown to fifty-five percent. In 1987, sixty percent of the female labor force was married, compared to twenty-three percent in 1920. Furthermore, despite the flood of stories in the popular press about successful educated women fleeing the corporate world for babies in the suburbs, every set of numbers from the Bureau of Labor Statistics shows the number of working mothers going up. In early 1988, sixty-five percent of college-educated women between the ages of twenty-five and forty-four, with a child under the age of six, were working. Among all women with small children, half are now in the labor force, compared with only thirty-one percent in 1975. Single parent mothers are more likely to be in the labor force than married ones, and black mothers are working at a higher rate than white mothers. For most women, working is a necessity, and families are dependent upon their wages; but in recent surveys, American women have indicated that they prefer a life that includes both family and work.[47]

This accelerated demand for employment is both the cause and effect of other far-reaching transformations in women's life patterns. Feminist historian Linda Gordon has explained how the restructuring of the labor force leads to a series of other important changes:

Increased women's employment means that adult couples, though not necessarily parent-child ties, are losing their economic necessity and women are becoming more reluctant to accommodate themselves to male privileges. Women's growing consciousness of themselves as workers will strengthen their sense of equality with men of their own class and stimulate resistance to their continued sexual exploitation by men.... No other variable seems to provide such a direct incentive to birth-control use, in all classes and ethnic groups, as women's employment.[48]

Women in the 1920s had access to the technology of birth control, but did not have an ideology which supported its use. Current demographic statistics show that as women's vocational and educational options have expanded, women have been able to make real decisions about their personal and reproductive lives as well.

Nevertheless, the recent advances and new opportunities for women in the working world have not solved many of the most serious problems identified in the 1920s. The great majority of women are still concentrated in traditionally female, low-paying occupations. Women are still ninety-nine percent of the secretaries, but only one percent of the auto mechanics; ninety-eight percent of the kindergarten and preschool teachers, but only thirty-six percent of the college and university professors. Although the earnings gap between men and women has improved slightly, in 1986 women workers earned only sixty-four percent of what their male counterparts made. Today only twenty-two percent of women workers are unionized, compared to about three percent in the 1920s, although there is evidence of less pay discrimination in unionized industries. Finally, despite the increasing presence of mothers in the work force, few employers offer child care or flexible scheduling. The conditions that would make it easier to combine work and family lives are yet a dream for most American women.

Thus we cannot blame the women of the 1920s for failing to create a feminist revolution. Many of the issues of the contemporary women's liberation movement—from job discrimination, to sex-role conditioning, to marriage contracts, to birth control—were raised in the 1920s. The *Nation* women experimented boldly and courageously with new life-styles and new careers. But they were a small minority of all American women, and they saw their problems as personal difficulties rather than as the effects of wider political problems. They did not have an analysis of social structures that allowed them to make connections between gender, race, and class.

The experience of women in the 1920s should not discourage us today. Even in the face of obstacles, even when the Great Depression wiped out many of the meager economic gains of the previous decade, American women did not give up and go home. The long struggle for women's freedom is far from over, but we distort our history if we believe that there were periods in which women deliberately gave their freedom away. At worst, the 1920s were indeed an "awkward age," a period of retreat and postponement. But the longings for independence, for strength and autonomy, for adventure and for service, which the *Nation* women express, and the suffragists had fought for, survived. In the 1930s, Lorine Pruette summed up the experience of her generation in a rewriting of the fable of Atalanta, who finally loses the race and marries the man who has defeated her:

After they were married Atalanta said nothing at all about all those other races which she had won, although she heard a great deal about the one that she had lost. She never told that she had grown weary of winning them, nor that she could see no real reason why she should take great pains to arrive always first at the myrtle tree, nor did she ever deny that the golden apples which were brought her on all future occasions were her favorite fruit. And when her husband competed in other races she came and cheered for him, until presently she forgot that she had been the fleetest runner on any island in the sea. But when upon that first smiling morning after her wedding Atalanta's old nurse had chid her because she had lost the race which she could certainly have won, had she cared enough, even though she had paused to gather all the apples, Atalanta put her quickly out of the room as she whispered finally, "Do not think that I was vanquished—I was diverted."[49]

Women in the 1920s were diverted, but not vanquished; and they taught their daughters to work for the time when the golden apples of love, family, and security would not come at the price of losing the race.

NOTES

1. *The Nation*, November 2, 1924, p. 523.

2. Dorothy Dunbar Bromley, "Feminist—New Style," *Harper's*, CLV (October 1927), pp. 552-60.

3. Quoted in June Sochen, *Movers and Shakers: American Women Thinkers and Activists, 1900-1970* (New York: Quadrangle, 1973), p. 51.

4. Phyllis Blanchard and Carolyn Manasses, *New Girls for Old* (New York, 1930); quoted in William O'Neill, *Everyone Was Brave: The Rise and Fall of Feminism in America* (Chicago: Quadrangle, 1969), p. 307.

5. Sochen, *Movers and Shakers*, p. 134. See also obituary notice, *New York Times*, January 4, 1976. Freda Kirchwey's papers are in the Schlesinger Library at Radcliffe College.

6. "The Pan American Conference of Women," *The Nation*, May 10, 1922, p. 565; quoted in Sochen, *Movers and Shakers*, p. 137.

7. Mary Ross, "New Status of Women in America," in V.F. Calverton and Samuel Schmalhausen, *Woman's Coming of Age* (New York: 1931), p. 538.

8. Lois Banner, *Women in Modern America* (New York: Harbrace, 1974), p. 108. See also Hutchins Hapgood, *A Victorian in the Modern World* (New York, 1939), pp. 332ff. A scrapbook presented by Club members to Marie Howe, "Heterodoxy to Marie," is in the collection of the Schlesinger Library.

9. For statistics on women in the 1920s, see Banner, *Women in Modern America*; William H. Chafe, *The American Woman: Her Changing Social, Economic, and Political Role* (New York: Oxford University Press, 1972); Peter G. Filene, *Him/Her/Self* (New York: Harcourt, Brace, Jovanovich, 1974); Estelle B. Friedman, "The New Woman: Changing Views of Women in the 1920s," *Journal of American History*, LXI (September 1974), pp. 372-393; Stanley Lemons, *The Woman Citizen: Social Feminism in the 1920s* (Urbana: University of Illinois Press, 1973); and Frank Stricker, "Cookbooks and Law Books: The Hidden Life of Career Women in Twentieth-Century America," *Journal of Social History*, X (Fall 1976), pp. 1-19.

10. See Lemons, *The Woman Citizen*, p. 180.

11. Blanchard and Manasses, *New Girls for Old*, p. 244.

12. O'Neill, *Everyone Was Brave*, p. 268.

13. *Ibid.*, p. 269.

14. *Ibid.*, p. 266.

15. "Here Are Ladies," *The Nation*, July 9, 1924, p. 42.

16. Chafe, *The American Woman*, p. 30.

17. *Ibid.*, p. 29.

18. "Should Men be Protected?" *The Nation*, August 31, 1927, p. 200.

19. Chafe, *The American Woman*, p. 102.

20. Alice Beal Parsons, "Man-made Illusions About Women," in Calverton and Schmalhausen, *Woman's Coming of Age*, p. 23.

21. Suzanne LaFollette, *Concerning Women* (New York: Albert and Charles Bond, 1926), p. 270.

22. Pruette, "The Married Woman and the Part-Time Job," *Annals of the American Academy of Political and Social Science*, CXLIII (May 1929), p. 302.

23. *Our Changing Morality* (New York: Albert and Charles Bond, 1924), pp. viii-ix.

24. Lorine Pruette, "Why Women Fail," in Calverton and Schmalhausen, *Woman's Coming of Age,* p. 255.

25. See Carroll Smith-Rosenberg, "The Female World of Love and Ritual: Relations Between Women in Nineteenth-Century America," *Signs,* I (1975), pp. 1-29.

26. Ann D. Gordon, Mari Jo Buhle, Nancy E. Schrom, "Women in American Society: An Historical Contribution," *Radical America,* V (1973).

27. Smith-Rosenberg, "The Female World of Love and Ritual," p. 27.

28. Mary Austin, "The Forward Turn," *The Nation,* July 20, 1927. P. 58.

29. Gordon, Buhle, Schrom, "Women In American Society," p. 48.

30. Elizabeth Kemper Adams, *Women Professional Workers* (New York: Macmillan, 1921), p. 438.

31. June Sochen, *The New Woman in Greenwich Village 1910-1920* (New York: Quadrangle, 1972), pp. 49-50.

32. Virginia Pope, *New York Times,* November 1, 1925; quoted in Alice Beal Parsons, *Women's Dilemma* (New York: Crowell, 1926), p. 211.

33. Anne Firor Scott, *The Southern Lady: From Pedestal to Politics 1830-1930* (Chicago: University of Chicago Press, 1970), p. 219.

34. On nonsupportive husbands, see "Confessions of an Ex-Feminist," *New Republic,* April 14, 1926, pp. 218ff. and Worth Tuttle, "Autobiography of an Ex-Feminist," *The Atlantic,* CLII (December 1933), p. 645.

35. Mary Alden Hopkins, "Fifty-Fifty Wives," *Woman Citizen,* VII (April 1, 1923), p. 12.

36. Pruette, "Why Women Fail," pp. 256-57.

37. Parsons, *Woman's Dilemma,* p. 247.

38. See Linda Gordon, *Woman's Body, Woman's Right: A Social History of Birth Control in America* (New York: Viking/Grossman, 1976).

39. One study showed that 90 out of 100 women with careers were easily able to find full-time servants to care for their children and homes. Virginia MacMakin Collier, *Marriages and Careers: A Study of One Hundred Women Who Are Wives, Mothers, Homemakers and Professional Women* (New York: The Channel Bookshop, 1926); see Banner, *Women in Modern America,* p. 154.

40. Evelyn Seeley, "Editing for Tomorrow," *Independent Woman,* 16 (November 1937), p. 357; quoted in Sochen, *Movers and Shakers,* p. 135.

41. See Frank Stricker, "Cookbooks and Law Books," pp. 10-11.

42. Pruette, "Why Women Fail," pp. 257-258.

43. Lucille Birnbaum, "Behaviorism in the 1920s," *American Quarterly,* VI (1955), pp. 15-30.

44. *Ibid.,* p. 18.

45. Nathan G. Hale, Jr., *Freud and the Americans* (New York: Oxford University Press, 1971), p. 275.

46. Susan Bolotin, "Voices from the Post-Feminist Generation," *New York Times Magazine,* 17 October 1982, pp. 28-31, 103, 106-7, 114, 116-17.

47. "Poll of U.S. Women Shows Jobs Rival Family Life," *New York Times,* Sunday, 4 December 1983, p. 66.

48. Linda Gordon, *Woman's Body, Woman's Right*, p. 142.

49. Pruette, "Why Women Fail," p. 259.

THE
ESSAYS

INEZ HAYNES IRWIN

Inez Haynes Irwin (1873-1970) was a well-known suffragist, journalist, and novelist. Hardly "the most timid of created beings," as she calls herself in her essay, she was a rebellious and daring woman, whose exciting life encompassed many of the radical themes of the modern era. Her own account of the militant suffrage movement and her views on the history of American women can be found in two of her books, *The Story of the Woman's Party* (1921), and *Angels and Amazons: A Hundred Years of American Women* (1933). In addition, Irwin had worked as fiction editor of *The Masses*, a major leftist periodical; and with her first husband, newspaper editor Rufus H. Gillmore, had traveled in prewar Europe meeting Russian revolutionaries, French impressionist painters, and American expatriates including Gertrude Stein. During World War I, Irwin was a war correspondent in France, England, and Italy. Her lively diaries and a manuscript autobiography are among her papers in the Schlesinger Library at Radcliffe College.

Beatrice M. Hinkle, one of the three psychologists who commented on this series in 1927, said about the author of "The Making of a Militant":

From the account of the family background it is evident that there was an atmosphere in the home of free discussion and a liberal attitude toward women's aspirations. There were women members of the household whose attitude was apparently distinctly modern, and therefore she imbibed during her youth the special nutriment which stimulated the individualistic aspect of her personality. Her exultation over the "first brick thrown" in the militant suffrage cause was a joyous release to action through the psychological mechanism of identification with the thrower, for she was thus enabled to overcome her personal timidity through a collective action.

Certainly Irwin was influenced by her family's background of New England intellectualism and by the personalities of her unusual parents. Her father, Gideon Haynes, changed careers several times, and Inez was born in Rio de Janeiro at the nadir of his business fortunes. When he returned to Boston and managed hotels, the family finances improved. Her mother, twenty-four years younger than her father, was his second wife and took over a family of seven children. She had ten children of her own; twelve of the combined family survived to adulthood. When Irwin writes of lovely young women marrying and becoming slaves to huge families, she is undoubtedly thinking of her own mother. And yet the Hayneses' marriage was not just the "makeshift matrimony" of an earlier generation; it was loving and intense. When Gideon Haynes died, his wife committed suicide.

As a child, Irwin had quickly recognized the differences between her opportunities and privileges, and those of her brothers. She longed for an adventurous life, for the "scarlet-and-gold country of the foot-loose male." Women's lives struck her as secondary and drab. In an article on "The Life of the Average Woman," written in 1912, Irwin imagined woman as "a slim, weak, pale, bowed, weary figure—weak, humorless, inarticulate, standing timidly on the threshold of life, peering through the open door, but not daring to enter." In an effort to escape forever from the contingency of womanhood, Irwin rejected much of the female culture of her generation.

Although Gillmore supported her efforts at independence and encouraged her both to attend Radcliffe as a special student and later to write, they were divorced. She married the journalist Will Irwin in 1916, and this was an immensely satisfying marriage. In the 1930s, Irwin began a popular series of children's books, the *Maida* stories. These fables emphasized the psychological destructiveness of the feminine mystique and stressed the value of hard work, usefulness, and independence. At the beginning of the series, Maida Westabrook is a melancholy invalid whose rich father (her mother is dead) has bought her everything from a life-size dollhouse to a railroad car, in a futile effort to restore her energy and spirits. Finally the family doctor realizes that Maida is suffering from her passivity and uselessness: " 'It isn't anything you can give her,' Dr. Pierce said impatiently; 'you must find something for her to do.'" Maida gives up her identity and goes with her Irish nanny to run a little shop in a poor section in Charleston, where eventually hard work and the stimulating contact with social reality cure her: "The consciousness of a new strength and a new power made a different child of her."

For Inez Irwin, being a modern woman meant being strong, active, and responsible, and no luxury could compensate for the freedom she had achieved for herself.

The Making of a Militant

I come from the oldest American stock. I can say that with absolute truth and without implication of snobbery because one of my ancestors, on my father's side, was an Indian girl. On my father's side we are English and Scotch back to 1636, when his first ancestor in this country came from England. On my mother's side, we are, with the exception of an Irish great-grandmother, of unmixed English blood, straight back through a signer of the Declaration of Independence to an ancestor on the Mayflower. It is, I believe, my father's blood—a long line of farmers—which has most influenced my thinking and is responsible for a kind of militant idealism which marks many of my family. It is, I believe, my mother's blood—a long line of mill-workers and mill-owners—which has most influenced me aesthetically. That strain has given me an intense love of beauty; a feeling, more poignant perhaps, when beauty is expressed in color rather than form.

There are two stories, hang-overs from the Revolutionary period in my father's family history, which always glow in my imagination. One is the story of a woman and the other of a man. The woman was the wife of my direct ancestor of that period. On the morning of April 19, 1775, her husband was plowing. Suddenly a man on a sweating horse stopped on the road in front of the house and yelled to him: "To arms! To arms! The regulars are coming!" My ancestor dropped his plow, rushed into the house, put on his coat, seized his musket, and ran down to the road. Once there, it occurred to him that he had not said goodby to his wife. He turned to wave to her—she had already taken his place at the plow.

The other story concerns the same battle. Deacon Josiah, one of my collateral ancestors, followed the British for miles along the line of fighting. That night he did not return. The next day he was found dead behind a stone wall. He had shot his last bullet, for there was not one left in his pouch. He was eighty years old.

Those stories made a profound impression on me. Sometimes I have wondered if they were not the real reason why for years I—naturally the most timid of created beings—was always in one civic fight at least; often in two; sometimes in more.

My early life was passed in Boston. I received the education typical of the upper middle-class in Massachusetts a generation ago. I went to four public schools—primary, grammar, high school, and normal school. I went to Radcliffe College. We were poor; genteelly poor; not poor enough to live in the slums and to know the thrill of haphazard picturesque slum existence, but poor enough to float along at a dead level of a lamb-stew existence. Yet the family life was informed with that idea of plain living and high thinking which was the New England ideal fifty years ago. As I look back on my life, it seems to be bound by the Boston *Transcript*, the Boston Public Library, the Boston Symphony, and the *Atlantic Monthly*.

I am one of seventeen children—the progeny of two wives and one father. The lives of all those children, except three who died in infancy, would make novels. I can here give but a carved cherry-stone idea of my own.

My father was born in 1815. He remembered with perfect clearness sitting as a boy in the chimney corner, listening to the tales of the Revolution told by men who had fought in it, and to discussions of witchcraft by people who still believed in witches. Clearly, too, he remembered when at eight his father took him to Charlestown to see the laying of the corner-stone of the Bunker Hill monument. Lafayette spoke on this occasion, and Daniel Webster. My father was a handsome person, the black-haired, olive-skinned, gray-eyed type, with a figure like a blade of Damascus steel, romantic, chivalrous, gallant, gay— *dashing* was the word they used to describe him. When he was a half-grown lad, he used to walk a distance—roughly of fifteen miles— into Boston to purchase the Waverley novels as fast as they appeared; trudged the fifteen miles back. As a youth, he went on the stage. It was his boast that he played every minor Shakespearean part, and that he had danced with Fanny Ellsler. He and a half-dozen other young men formed themselves into a black-face company and went to England; the first to visit Albion's shores. This was in 1844. They used to tramp from town to town giving their show and then moving on. My father made pilgrimages to the homes of Shakespeare and Byron, and to all the places he could identify that Scott had mentioned in his Waverley novels. He had a picturesque career; as prison reformer—he was, so far as I know, the first prison reformer in this country—politician, lecturer, author, and traveler. As he grew older, that fire of his youth toned down to an extraordinary quiet. Always an agnostic, he became a confirmed pessimist, but a gentle and humorous one; he seemed to develop an extraordinary wisdom.

My mother was twenty-four years younger than my father, beautiful in a delicately robust way; temperamentally capricious; illogical; vain with that charming vanity of the mid-Victorian epoch. All these youngnesses were illumined by a natural instinct for beauty; and they were held together by a dominant quality, seemingly alien to the combination—common sense.

She was one of a large family of girls. Her mother died when she was ten. Her father immediately married again—the makeshift matrimony of a man left alone with an unsolvable problem. My mother brought herself up. Early she went to work in the mills which were owned by her uncles, and in which their relatives were both foremen and workers. It was the Lucy Larcom period in American industry; all my mother's fellow-workers were women of American birth. And there was no sense of social inferiority in working in a mill. One day, perhaps, some American novelist will reconstruct that interesting epoch. I remember her telling us that the year she was eighteen she hired a horse on the Fourth of July, and in a habit which she had made for herself rode from Lowell to Boston—to see the doings on Boston Common. When she was seventeen my mother heard my father make a speech. She came home, waked up all her sisters, and kept them laughing half the night in spirited girlish imitations of him. The next year she met him. A few months later they were married. He placed her immediately at the head of a large household, where life moved in a highly romantic manner. In winter she used daily to skate. This frivolity in a married woman appalled the close, conservative community in which she lived. She used to ride horseback almost up to the time her babies were born. And this appalled them even further. Subsequently my father lost his fortune, tiny for this day, but ample for those—and the bad times came. It was at their nadir that I was born; and my youth saw no amelioration of them.

Yet ours was a big family and an extremely gay one.

Two aunts were familiars of our household. One, my father's younger sister, was a remarkable person. She had been a school-teacher. At the age of fifty-odd she was offered the place of a man principal who had just resigned from the school in which she taught. However, when she discovered that she was expected to do all his work but would not receive anything like his salary, she refused the job. She entered a theological seminary, was graduated at the head of the class, the only woman in it—one of the first American women clergymen. She had a parish in each of two towns, north of Boston. She preached in one church Sunday morning and the other Sunday night. When she was over seventy she retired; returned to her native town. A year later a delegation of farmers waited on her and asked her to come back, naming any salary within reason.

The second household familiar, also my father's sister, was a strong spiritualist. For four summers in my teens I went with her to a spiritualist camp-meeting in Massachusetts. Every morning and after-noon there were lectures in what they called the "auditorium." There was absolutely nothing for a young person to do in the camp-meeting; and so, out of sheer ennui, I attended all those lectures. Looking back, it seems to me, I heard discussed there every possible system of ethics, every possible theory of humanitarianism. I was a passive creature. These drifts of thought seemed to float over my mind without touching it. I was conscious then of no impression. I realize now that they had a profound effect.

However, I was accustomed to hear all kinds of discussions between my father and my two aunts. My mother, who bore no direct part in the discussion, was always flashing into their abstractions the strong flare of her common sense, the sparkle of her mother-wit. From an early age I became used to ideas. I was at home with them. I don't remember ever having to think things out when new ideas were presented to me. I knew instantly whether I accepted them as truth or not. With an exception; one of the strongest convictions of my thinking life, feminism, was a gradual growth. Indeed, I don't remember hearing the word feminism until I got to college.

In regard, however, to that tiny practical aspect of feminism—the franchise for women—I became very early an instant and ardent disciple. The question was first put to me by an extremely able woman teacher in the grammar school. Immediately my mind accepted as truth the idea that women should become in the fullest sense—citizens. I remember taking my new-found theory to my clergyman aunt, thinking I was going to open up a new vista to her. "I have believed in woman's rights all my life," she commented tranquilly. "And so has your father." From that time on, with increasing closeness, I was to be connected with the suffrage fight—that long-drawn-out, all-absorbing, irritating, boring battle for an obviously just and tiny bit of human liberty. I became very impatient with the slowness of a struggle waged on such scrupulously polite lines, and when the first militant in England threw the first brick my heart flew with it. Thereafter I was a firm believer in militant tactics. Toward the end of the movement I was identified with the militant wing of the suffrage fight.

But although this struggle seemed to occupy the surface of my mind, I was faintly conscious of a vague but deeper unrest underneath. Away back in the early stirrings of my young-girl thinking I became definitely conscious of a growing impatience with the woman's lot. From the moment I was able to think for myself—and I suppose I could number on the fingers of one hand the women I have met in a lifetime who have not agreed with me—I regretted bitterly that I had not been born a man. Like all young things I yearned for romance and adventure. It was not, however, a girl's kind of romance and adventure that I wanted, but a man's. I wanted to run away to sea, to take tramping trips across the country, to go on voyages of discovery and exploration, to try my hand at a dozen different trades and occupations. I wanted to be a sailor, a soldier. I wanted to go to prize-fights; to frequent bar-rooms; even barber-shops and smoking-rooms seemed to offer a brisk, salty taste of life. I could not have been more than fourteen when I realized that the monotony and the soullessness of the lives of the women I knew absolutely appalled me.

This was, understand, life in the middle class. These were, understand, women without private means or without the capacity for earning money for themselves.

I saw that most of them enjoyed one brief period of budding and another of flowering; the romance periods of young love and early marriage. After that—my heart sank as I contemplated the picture. All about me I saw lovely young things marrying, producing an annual baby, taking care of too many children in the intervals of running their houses. It seemed to me that early they degenerated into one of two types: the fretful, thin, frail, ugly scold or the good-natured, fat, slatternly slut.

As I look back on those years, the mid-day Sunday dinner seemed in some curious way to symbolize everything that I hated and dreaded about the life of the middle-class woman. That plethoric meal—the huge roast, the blood pouring out of it as the man of the house carved; the many vegetables, all steaming; the heavy pudding. And when the meal was finished—the table a shambles that positively made me shudder—the smooth replete retreat of the men to their cushioned chairs, their Sunday papers, their vacuous nap, while the women removed all vestiges of the horror. Sunday-noon dinners! They set a scar upon my soul. I still shudder when I think of them.

A profound horror of the woman's life filled me. Nothing terrified me so much as the thought of marriage and child-bearing. Marriages seemed to me, at least so far as women were concerned, the cruelest of traps. Yet most women married and all seemed to want to marry. Those who remained single often changed into something more repellent than those charmless drudges. I made all kinds of resolutions against matrimony. All the time, though, I was helplessly asking myself, how was I going to fight it—when I so loved companionship?

One way, I decided, was not to let myself get caught in any of those pretty meshes which threaten young womanhood. I made a vow that I would never sew, embroider, crochet, knit—especially would I never learn to cook. I made a vow that if those things had to be done, I would earn the money to pay for them. I married, but I kept my vow. I have always paid for them. Even in a young marriage, when income was very limited, I went without clothes to keep a maid. And although I happen to be extremely domestic in that I must have a home and much prefer to stay in it, I have always managed that the work of that home should be done by someone else, and that my clothes should be made outside it.

Through all this spiritual turmoil there had been developing within me a desire to write. And during all these years, I was making a tentative experiment with the august business of reflecting the life about me. Ultimately my first short story was accepted; more short stories; a book; more books. Except for three or four years, my mature life has been economically independent. I hope to be economically independent the rest of my days. When I look back on my fifty-odd years of life on this planet, I wonder what was the real inception of my desire to stand alone—fighting ancestry; liberal influences; discussion-ridden youth? Perhaps it was those Sunday dinners!

MARY ALDEN HOPKINS

Mary Alden Hopkins (1876-1960) was born in Bangor, Maine, and educated at Wellesley College and Columbia University, where she received an M.A. degree. Her father was a banker; her home style, "monogamous, Republican, and Protestant." In his comment on the series, psychologist Joseph Collins found Hopkins one of the two women he would not have wanted to "companion," seeing in her essay "a childish sense of guilt. The grief and gloom of her parents was that they had brought her into the world and she has a passionate desire to be no trouble to her husband." But Hopkins had come to understand much more about her past than these facile psychoanalytic observations. Growing up, she realized that her parents' unhappiness, her mother's nervous prostration and semi-invalidism, came "as much from being married to each other" as from having to take care of her. Hopkins' wish to be independent was based on her observation of the discontented lives of dependent women.

When she finally broke away from her family, in the aftermath of a painful love affair, Hopkins tried to make up for lost time by immersing herself in radical activism. She became a staunch feminist, identifying with the suffering of working women and prostitutes. Her journalism included stories on the labor movement and research for the National Child Labor Commission, the Consumers League, and the Massachusetts Minimum Wage Commission. She also wrote fiction for the women's magazines and, in 1947, published her only book, *Hannah More and Her Circle*, a study of an eighteenth-century moralist.

Hopkins' essay is both bitter and disillusioned. She has lost her faith in protest and rebellion; "will it work?" has become her moral code. Recounting the story of her unhappy romance, her delayed career, she is nonetheless unable to connect her own experience to a political analysis of women's situation. Thus she tells us that no one was to blame for her blighted engagement, although her parents' disapproval clearly destroyed it; and she insists that it is "nobody's fault" that "men got the good jobs," and "virtuous women shriveled at their desks." Hopkins' hope that life will be easier for a younger generation seems uncertain.

Why I Earn My Own Living

For thirty years I walked primly, directing my course by the social guide-posts set up in a New England town for the direction of well-born, well-bred little ladies. Then I broke loose. My former friends consider me a sort of wild woman because I earn my own living, do not take my husband's name, and have been known to live in strange, dirty neighborhoods where the rents are lower. To myself I seem much the same person who used to leave properly engraved visiting-cards on proper occasions at proper houses.

I earn my living as a matter of course now, but the habit started from a childish sense of guilt at making my parents so much trouble. My mother took life rather hard. She was extremely sensitive to responsibility; she hated routine duties, but her conscience forced her to perform them scrupulously. Again and again she gave up the nerve-racking struggle and took to her bed, discovering nervous prostration long before it was recognized by the medical profession and taken up generally by distressed gentlewomen. Both she and I thought that taking care of me was what made her sick.

Like all children I was a complete egoist. My world revolved around myself and when it was a clouded world I assumed that I was to blame. There was always in the foreground some naughtiness like screaming against bed-time, demanding a toilet where there was none, refusing to wear a certain dress, or being impertinent. I could not comprehend that my parents' gloom came as much from being married to each other as from being my father and mother. Early in life I figured out that the least I could do for two people who had done so much for me was as soon as possible to earn my own living. I hoped thus to lessen my sense of guilt in living at all. Some of my playmates, now middle-aged, have tried to assuage a similar feeling in a different way; they have continued in their childhood homes instead of forming independent ties and their parents have become their children.

Later on, I carried over into my marriage the old, illusive sense of guilt and a passionate desire to be no trouble to my husband. I had the naive belief that men loved best women who were no bother to them. I had the curious idea that my husband would admire my power to earn money and be proud of my standing in my profession.

The working-for-wages habit was well established before I turned critical eyes on the courtship, engagement, and marriage customs of my town. In the large city where I had received a school appointment after graduating from college, I "poured" at "receptions," played atrocious bridge, went to dances, taught in Sunday school, and expected to marry a pleasant house with steam heat, electricity, and a husband. Until I was more than thirty years old I refrained from thoughts about sex because "there is time enough for that after you are married."

Through the printed word I escaped the dreary commonplace. The verses of Hovey, Carman, and Le Gallienne were my creed. I soaked up the saccharine art of the Pre-Raphaelites in English galleries and mooned about the English Lake district, tested life by the philosophy of Hall Caine and Marie Corelli, adored Maude Adams and Sothern (before he took to Shakespeare), and wrote diluted love lyrics.

The girls of my little group of young folks were all weltering in sentimentality, but they were mostly able to distinguish between reality and fantasy. The other girls didn't try to make an apple-pie by the rule for a sonnet. They wrapped their affections about young men who had what was called "character" in distinction to "personality." After marriage they discarded romantic fancies and stagnated in mild discontent. But I had only one foot firmly planted on solid respectability; the other was sliding round on romance. You recognize this situation as what we now name "a conflict of desires."

The romantic side of my nature led me to pick out a charming man in the city where I was teaching. Or did he pick me out? I do not know; it was love at first sight; and, looking back, I would not have missed it for the world. The practical side of my nature compelled me to take him home to my parents to be approved. They refused their approbation. The man had been divorced, he was a Socialist, and had been brought up as a Catholic. My home circle was monogamous, Republican, and Protestant. One marriage, one political party, one church were the portion of one individual in those days.

My parents declined to accept my man as a son-in-law. I would not marry him without their consent because "a bad daughter makes a bad wife"; yet I wouldn't give him up because life without him was too utterly dreary. The outcome was that he went back to the city to make a fortune as a substitute for "character," while I returned to teach school in my home town. In those days an engaged girl stayed with her parents during her engagement because she was so soon to leave them. I spent my leisure filling my Hope Chest. All my lingerie was made by hand. It took longer than we expected for my fiance to make a fortune and I watched myself grow older.

My man actually did make a fortune. But he married a woman who, I afterward learned, had been working and living with him during his long, hard pull. Everyone was satisfied but me. I was mad clear through. I had been a good daughter and had lost my lover thereby. I had no desire to be anything but good, but I did not want to be punished for it. Reviewing the affair, I could not see that anyone was to blame. The code had let me down.

Then and there I renounced allegiance to ready-made codes. I again left my home town and went away to work out my salvation or destruction. I had to be free to study what had happened to me and to figure out a working plan for my life. Being self-supporting I was able to move about. Even now I do not like to recall the suffering of that period. For several years the world was a gray fog spinning about me. Every guide-post by which I had directed my course had been swept away. I had lost, not a lover but a universe.

Intense curiosity awoke in me. Always I had repressed questionings because they led to criticism of the fundamentals of society. The brain cannot function if it is not allowed to question, and my intelligence was as weak as that of a new-born babe. I got a job reading in libraries, gathering material for a writer. Seven hours a day I put in on the assigned subjects and the rest of the time I read about anarchy, sex, votes-for-women, education, divorce, and similar topics. I read till my eyes puffed out and my head was splitting. I went to university lectures and also met soap-box orators. I gobbled ideas.

Books were not enough. I went in for people, plunged headforemost into crowds. I lived in a tenement, worked in factories, and went to meetings and meetings and meetings. The sweat, the vulgarity, the commonness of humans in the bulk were both a horror and a pleasure to me. I experimented conscientiously with being "wicked," and was keenly disappointed to find so little excitement in sinning and so little sense of guilt.

The driving emotion of that period of my life was curiosity. I was insatiable concerning every subject with which I came in contact. I even got jobs to investigate wages, prostitution, fire-escapes. Because I had known so little I wanted to know everything. I prowled the world like a cat on the housetop. Along with curiosity went pity. My own suffering had opened my eyes to the suffering all about me. Working conditions, living arrangements, the general social code seemed to me extraordinarily stupid. I discovered that I was not the only woman uncomfortable in the world. The office charwoman's cracked hands were dyed brown from washing filthy floors; growing girls lugged heavy babies about the playgrounds; prostitutes complained because they had to hand over their earnings to pimps; virtuous women shriveled at their desks; men got the good jobs.

I flung my puny strength into the fight for social legislation. Occasionally the group with which I worked got some well-intentioned law passed, but immediately a new condition arose which was different but quite as intolerable. My reaction to the suffering which I could not assuage was similar to my attitude toward my broken heart; since I could do nothing about it, I would pass on.

I reacted violently at that time against all established institutions, like marriage, spanking, meat diet, prisons, war, public schools, and our form of government. The mere fact that a condition existed was evidence to me that it was wrong. Yet as I watched the lives of those radicals who dared live their rebellion, the rebels appeared to get no more satisfaction than did the conformists and smugness seemed equally common among both extremes. I did some experimenting myself, and never have I found any completely satisfactory arrangement of financial, social, or personal relationships. The wise course now seems to me to decide what one wants, whether one can get it, whether or not it is worth the price that must be paid, and then to go after it. "Will it work?" is my moral code.

Although I supported myself in the beginning because I thought it was my duty it has become a matter of course. I have no principles on the subject but I perfer money-earning to being dependent on a father, a lover, or a husband. Dependent women seem hampered even more than wage-earning ones. Likewise I hold no brief for or against marriage, having tried celibacy, free union, and marriage.

I do not know what woman's job in life is, any more than I know what man's job is. And I feel it is rather silly to drag sex into the matter. My journalistic career, the fact that I have turned to account in printed word and cold cash the curiosity that drove me in my groping middle years, is the source of a certain pride and self-confidence which is the springboard for my future. Now, at forty-odd, I stand where the young man of thirty stands, with enough solid achievement behind me to nourish an ambition to do still bigger things. I see quite plainly that it is the fact of my being a woman which has delayed me fifteen years in reaching this point. It is nobody's fault; I was born in circumstances which our generation has helped to destroy. The younger women seem able to get away to a start without so much muddling.

SUE SHELTON WHITE

Sue Shelton White (1887-1943), southern leader of the National Woman's Party, lawyer, and Democratic party politician, is usually regarded by historians as a "public feminist," committed to women's issues from a political and civic perspective. But this essay, unknown to her previous biographers, shows how primary, personal, and deep her feminist affiliations and attitudes were. In many details, her story resembles that of the other lawyer in the Nation series, Crystal Eastman. Both women strongly identified with their resourceful mothers. Both had fathers who were ministers. Unlike Crystal Eastman's mother, however, Sue White's mother was not accepted by her husband's parish. When he died, she struggled to support her children through a variety of marginal jobs. The Whites' children, like the Eastmans', shared the household tasks without regard to sex. When Sue White was thirteen, her mother died; she was reared by an aunt and an older sister. In some sense, her whole life was a defense of a woman's right to be herself, a right to which her mother's life bore witness.

In 1907, White became a court reporter in Jackson, Tennessee, a position she kept for eleven years, seeing "many aspects of life that provided good training for a feminist." In 1918, she became chairwoman of the Tennessee branch of the Woman's Party and then editor of the *Suffragist*, the party's official publication. White's connection with the militant suffragists of the Woman's Party and her participation in their demonstrations in Washington (she served five days in the District Jail for burning a cartoon of President Wilson) probably hurt her later in her political career. But militancy was an important affirmation of autonomy, of the refusal to accept intimidation. White "found that almost unaware," she had committed herself to the struggle for women.

Her essay emphasizes the obstacles and prejudices she had to overcome at every stage of her career: the genteel limitations of southern ladyhood, the outright discrimination against women, and, finally, the flattery of tokenism. Fighting to become a lawyer (she got her degree at the age of thirty-six) and to make a place for herself in the Democratic party hierarchy, she bitterly recognized how many problems women faced beyond the Nineteenth Amendment. As she wrote to her friend and fellow Democrat, Mary Dewson, in 1928, "Women have been discouraged by the rank and file of the party organization. . . . And the few women who have been artificially reared up as leaders are not leaders of women and have been reared not to lead women but to fool them" (Anne Firor Scott, *The Southern Lady*, p. 206).

Generally, however, White was not bitter, but active and positive. For many years she worked with Dewson, Nellie Taylor Ross, and Eleanor Roosevelt in organizing Democratic party women, and in the 1930s, she served on the legal staff of the new Social Security Board. Choosing not to marry, she recognized that "renunciation too is a lopping-off." But the spirit of her essay is not sadness and renunciation; it is the strength gained from her "single-handed grappling with life."

Mother's Daughter

A Methodist preacher smote the cheek of his presiding elder several years before I was born. After that my father's preaching terminated abruptly.

It was about my mother's right to be herself. The Methodist brethren wanted to force my mother into the Methodist church, an intimidation to which my father would not or could not be a party.

They met about 1870 when she was 18 and he was 29. She was teaching, and had been teaching for four years, in a little town near the mouth of the Ohio River. He came from a nearby State to teach in the same school. Girls usually married early in those days, when they had a chance, but my mother temporized about marriage for five years, teaching all the while. She married at 23, and continued to teach. Wherever the church sent my father, she taught. She was not a Methodist, but they worked together constantly; she went with him into the work of church and schoolroom, into his Sunday schools, into his mission. She may have helped him with his sermons. But she did not join his church.

Eventually they found themselves in a rabidly intolerant Southern Methodist community. Here my mother was baited and harassed because of her adherence to her good old Baptist faith. Then, too, children came, and it was doubtless embarrassing to the Methodist brethren to have their own minister's babies crawl around unsprinkled and to have their own minister's wife avoid partaking of the Methodist communion. One thing led to another and to the final break. Of course father might have asserted himself more. He might have slapped his wife rather than his presiding elder and thus held on to his frock. He did none of these things.

So Methodist and Baptist they remained, but outside of the ministry. They were Democrats, too, and consistent in a moderate Southernism. He was the son of a slaveholding planter who had lost everything in the war. She was from "immigrant" non-slaveholding stock, with little to lose. We were poor. Life was a struggle and religion a comfort. My parents believed in God, of course—the Father, Son, and Holy Ghost—and in the Resurrection Day. Nevertheless, during the six years I knew my father, I heard him swear occasionally. He indulged in tobacco, and now and then a toddy. My mother tried to teach me the steps of the dances of her girlhood. She and my father had attended opera in New Orleans. I heard him say I might become an opera singer if I held my lung-power—perhaps a Jenny Lind. One of my brothers was permitted to have a deck of cards. Checkers and parchesi and dominoes were not denied us—even on Sunday. A collection of Arabian Nights tales was in our book-case and I read it early and had the stories told me at an even more tender age. There were also Shakespeare, Carlyle, Tom Paine, Victor Hugo, and George Eliot—who, my mother told me, "was really a woman named Mary Ann Evans."

My mother drew few distinctions between her boys and girls. I have seen my brothers sweep, wipe dishes, and even cook. I had four brothers, three older and one younger. The attitude of my older brothers was friendly rather than merely protective. I followed them around, but not everywhere—not to school nor to "town" nor hunting nor fishing. But I was permitted to "help" load shells, dig worms, and make kites. I imitated them and was applauded. I learned to turn somersaults, "skin the cat," and stand on my head. I knew these things were not for public exhibition, but I do not remember who told me so or what reasons were given. By the time I was nine or ten years old I had developed into something of a tomboy. Then one of my brothers died and the other two went away.

My younger brother was frail, sensitive, and imaginative. As he was almost four years younger and not as strong and healthy as I was, my relations with him were almost the reverse of my relations with my older brothers. So I was not subdued. Perhaps I was trying to be to him what they had been to me. I became even more tomboyish and finally assumed an active physical superiority over my younger brother and over my sister, who was bookish. If they excelled me in some things, I knew where I could excel. I ran, jumped, climbed, and, not infrequently, fought.

The town in which we lived was new and on a new railroad. My father surveyed the site, but the town straggled along rather whimsically without regard to his plans. Our house stood near the center— on my father's map; but, as a matter of fact, it stood in the twilight zone between the main town and the Negro settlement known as "Jaybird." What had been planned as the street in front of the house became a yellow line of mud or dust with a plank walk on one side, leading to the road which was the beginning of Main Street. So, while a part of the town, we were isolated. If I sought playmates outside of my family I usually had to go across town to them or induce them to come across town to me. I played with both boys and girls. One of my playmates was the grandson of a neighbor. I did not realize that he was stupid as long as we were just playing. When I saw him at school I became ashamed of him, because he could not learn. So much of my study had been done at home that I had had little opportunity to make comparisons, but at school I looked about me, at playmates, class-mates, and then at my books. I discovered that there were degrees of intelligence lower than my own. The tomboy began to recede and the star-pupil to emerge.

After my older brothers left home, most of the out-of-door chores fell to me. I brought in the wood and coal, carried water from the well, cut the kindling, made the fires and ran errands. I also learned to cook such simple food as we had. I went barefoot through the hot months. My mother had rather large feet and wore shoes to fit them. She talked about the foolishness of women who bound their feet and waists. She wore corsets occasionally, but she often tried to avoid them by sewing stays into her basques. She was slender. When I grew to the corset age she ordered a "corset waist." I wore it loose—and I was then fat. I have never classed my mother as a feminist, but I suspect she was one. Life would have made her one in the end if she had not been in the beginning. After my father's death she faced the necessity of support-ing a large family—six of us—in a town of less than a thousand population. She taught and gave music lessons—"piano and voice." She sent local items to newspapers in nearby cities. She peddled pianos and sometimes books. Between these activities she supervised our studies, our reading, our behavior, our work; nursed her neighbors, laid out their dead, helped their children with their school essays, and was kind to the Negroes who lived in the little huts nearby. When the children of these Negroes showed a craving for "book-larnin' " as they sometimes did, she taught them. In her narrow, almost primitive field, she held her position as an unusual, if sometimes a troublesome, woman—always tolerated and sometimes acclaimed.

I am sure that there were times when my mother did not know whence the next week's food would come. One can understand how this struggle would have affected her attitude toward her daughters, even if her previous life had not shown her aversion to dependency. She fed our ambitions. She would have wanted us to go to college and to get degrees had she lived and been able to manage. A normal school was established in our town and people came to it from the swamps around and the farther hills. It was run by the Campbellites—calling them-selves "Christians." Each year this school held debates on the relative mental equipment of men and women. The debates usually lasted for a week and practically the whole student body took part. I managed to get into them in some way, if only by trying to help the other girls meet the onslaught of historical data. No feminist literature was available. We got our nitrogen out of the air.

I do not remember that I was a conscious feminist until long after my mother's death. As a child and a girl I simply lived as an individual with little knowledge of the world and its poison of sex-antagonism. I left school at fourteen, because of my mother's illness. When she died I had hardly emerged from childhood, and girlhood was all but dissolved in the emotional reaction from her death and the necessity that drove me forth. I went to work very soon, in order that I might eat. This much the world was willing that I do—if not too heartily or too fastidiously.

In the South innumerable families were in economic distress; and, underneath the social traditions, there was an almost clannish effort to regain economic power without sacrificing pride or prestige in the struggle. Women had their part to play in the scheme. "Ladies" went to work—at home if they could, or at "genteel" work on the outside. One might be pitied, but if one "belonged" one could join the ranks of genteel workers temporarily without suffering social stigma. Meanwhile the conventional feminine tradition remained undisturbed. This social-psychological phenomenon belonged to the early transition period, although it still hangs on here and there. One met it only where one was known. As time went on and the straitened ones got back on their economic feet, there was a change, a reaction. Lines were again drawn taut.

My childhood was not such as to give me a snob's viewpoint. I had always understood that if I went to a certain distant county where my grandfather had worked his slaves, I would "belong." But I did not go, except to visit. And I ignored the "genteel" limitations that would have preserved my status as a "lady." I studied stenography. For two years I worked with a company that manufactured articles of iron and steel and wood. There were machine shops, foundries, a carpenter's shop, and a place where pneumatic tools were turned against rivets. I wrote specifications—long lists of strange words. I studied catalogues to try to see what the words meant. I begged the foremen to take me through the shops. My interest was a nuisance and treated as such, although the interest of the office boy was encouraged as a laudable ambition to "learn the business." I was not there to learn the business but to type things. I asked my employer if he thought it would help me to take a correspondence course in mechanical engineering. He gave me a fatherly lecture on woman's sphere in life, her place in the business world.

I pointed my pencil toward the courthouse and became a "crack" court reporter. I was flattered by my lawyer friends as the wonder of the verbatim-shorthand world. I saved them a lot of work. But when I began to talk of studying law, they called me impractical and visionary. It was about time I was getting married, anyhow. I observed that young men were encouraged to "read." They were taken into offices, into the trial of cases, sponsored, even fed, sometimes, by the older members of the bar; and the banks would extend them credit while they were struggling. I had one friend more sympathetic than others, a judge who put his hand on the political wheel and turned it in my favor. He said to me: "Senator So-and-So says I can name his secretary and I am going to suggest you, so you can go to Washington and maybe find time to study law." The next day he came back. "They just would not stand for a woman; I could not make them see it." It was years before I studied law, years before I got to Washington, years before I saw a Senator's office. It wasn't much to see, when I reached there.

During my twelve years as a court reporter I saw many aspects of life that provided good training for a feminist. I heard some of the worst sex abnormalities defined and described; I heard dramatic stories of frustrations and misunderstandings. I saw the results in human terms of the legal disabilities of women. I turned to reading and encountered Ibsen, Shelley—and whom else? I remember a book by Bouck White, "The Call of the Carpenter," a revolutionary-Christian-feminist document—if one be in the mood to take the whole dose. I was in the mood at that time. Then one day I fell into an argument about suffrage. I found that almost unaware I had committed myself. I became a suffragist, an active one, finally a militant one. As I plunged deeper in the suffrage fight, I had to marshal all my defenses. Prejudices were strong. I fared better than some of my associates by virtue of the strength gained from my single-handed grappling with life. Men would sometimes say, "If all women were like you," and I had to learn to dismiss the flattery.

I have not married. I have had my chances—one of the first being a station agent who insisted on "giving me a home." I suspected that he needed assistance in checking freight bills at the depot. I have also had my disappointments—one especially. He is still singing in the choir and is president of a Kiwanis Club. Without regard to my register of eligibles, I believe I could not now be induced to enter into the present legal status of marriage. Perhaps the day will come when I shall make my peace with the conventions, submit to the law through a justice of the peace or even a bishop, and get married. I doubt it. Marriage is too much of a compromise; it lops off a woman's life as an individual. Yet the renunciation too is a lopping off. We choose between the frying-pan and the fire—both very uncomfortable.

4

ALICE MARY KIMBALL

Alice Mary Kimball, a journalist and poet, is the sort of woman contemporary feminists would call "male-identified." She was the child of a strong, responsible mother and a poetic, glamorous father, a man in the age-old model of the male radical, with "a poet's passion for the oppressed" and a fiery passion "against injustice in various forms"—as long as the oppression and the injustice lay at a comfortable distance from his own home. Kimball was aware that her mother's energy and labor as a schoolteacher paid for her father's romantic self-indulgence and that her parents' marriage was "incongruous and bitterly unhappy." But she never allowed her adult perceptions of her father's shortcomings and her mother's strength to interfere with her own romantic child's fantasy of Father as the source of beauty, excitement, love, and wisdom. Her own marriage (to Harry Godfrey) was satisfactory, she tells us, though her husband "does not measure up to the myth—no man could." In her professional work as a reporter she "dogged the footsteps of intellectual men," and her vision of the future included a "very, very great father" who would choose her to confide in.

Kimball grew up in the small town of Woodbury, Vermont, and like Genevieve Taggard, another poet-essayist with whom she had much in common, she used small-town America as the setting of her most powerful work. Educated at the Johnson State Normal School in Vermont, she married in 1914 and worked as a labor investigator, journalist, and New York City librarian. *The Devil is a Woman* (1929), a collection of Kimball's poems which first appeared in such important periodicals as *The American Mercury* and *The Liberator,* presents many affectionate portraits of village women. Life is bitter and hard for these women—for the hired girls who are seduced, for the mothers who yearn for a heaven where they can "rest a million years and do crochet," for the exhausted child-bearers who would rather see a daughter "a-lyin' in her coffin than married to any man above." "Stacia Whitsett" gets herself elected as Town Clerk with the support of a kind of grass-roots Women's Political Caucus:

> The women's clubs of Dorset.
> I've worked in them for years. I know their power.
> I can depend till death on Pansy Lyford,
> The strong-willed founder of the Civic Circle;
> And Emma Leete, the Temperance Union fighter;
> And Amy Treete, head of the Culture Circle;
> The chairman of the Bird Club, Jane Proudfoot,
> So white-haired and so wise and scholarly,
> And dean of women at the Seminary.

Kimball recognized that the women in these communities had a power of sisterhood which came out of the apparent insignificance of female culture. Although she does not mention her suffrage activities in her essay, she had been sentenced to fifteen days in the Washington District Jail for taking part in a militant suffrage demonstration in Lafayette Square in August 1918. Conditions in the prison were so primitive that the women decided to hunger strike, following the example of the British suffragettes. After five days they were released. In *Jailed for Freedom*, Doris Stevens describes them "trembling with weakness, some of them with chills and some of them in a high fever, scarcely able even to walk to the ambulance or motor car." When Alice Kimball quietly comments that she "no longer works on movements," we should recall that she had earned her retirement.

The Peacock's Tail

Mother aspired to have a home of her own free of mortgages, children who would grow up and settle near her, each in a home free of mortgages; and a solid place in the respect of the New England rural community where her ancestors felled primeval forests and slaughtered wolf-packs.

This ambition could have been realized almost without effort in the natural course of things had she not, ironically, wished also for a "smart" husband. This yearning was the only colored thread in the fabric of her make-up. She waited until her late twenties for Prince Charming, supporting herself by school-teaching. An oddity of sex-selection: this little brown hen of a woman, with pink cheeks and dark eyes, pecking modestly away, pretending to look only at the wheat-grains before her, and watching all the while for the multi-color of a peacock's tail.

Peacocks and exciting men are hard to find in the sterile back country of northern Vermont; but mother with a hard eye rejected the well-to-do and the dumb. Her reputation as a pedagogue and disciplinarian waxed as she marked time and looked through schoolhouse windows for the gleam of a poet's hair.

Life played a story-book trick. Into the drab neighborhood where she pounded the three R's into slow-witted heads came a romantic troubadour, the like of whom had never illuminated the place before or will again. He was a young man of twenty-one who was going through the country admiring the scenery, reading Keats under trees, and teaching neighborhood "singing schools" by night to pay his way. Photographs taken at the time show a tall, beautiful youth, with hair thrown back from an intellectual brow, a sensitive face, and eyes burning with—let us say genius, for so it seemed to mother. They were dark-blue eyes, expressive, glowing.

Mother knew what she wanted and lost no time in annexing it.

Alas, for the home free of mortgages, the building of a substantial family clan. These essentials in her picture of the good life she was never to have. She underwrote her genius husband while he tilted at windmills. He had to be financed through bar examinations, through the stage of getting a professional foothold. Clients were few and were largely under-dogs, for father had a poet's passion for the oppressed and a poet's dislike of being bored. He wrote fiery pamphlets protesting against injustice in various forms—for the printing of which mother paid.

Mother is rounding out this year a solid half century of school-teaching. Her six children were born prudently in vacation time. I came in the Christmas holidays, the first child of an incongruous and bitterly unhappy marriage.

I was physically backward and mentally precocious. "At the age of twelve months you were a fat, clumsy baby without a tooth, and you looked at your toys and poked them instead of playing with them. You would never build houses with blocks, but you began learning the alphabet from them when you were a year old. You would hold up blocks and ask questions about the pictures and letters. By the age of seventeen months you knew the alphabet, but you weren't so good at walking. You tumbled and got many bumps." So wrote mother when I asked her for details.

Mother wrote, too, that I was a sickly child, that my life, in its first few months, was despaired of. I was much dandled and hovered over. My father walked the floor with me night after night. Was this spoiling the beginning of the yeasty ego, the Luciferian pride which makes me hanker for a superman?

I want a man like my father! Not like father as he actually was, but like father as he seemed in the first eight or ten years of my life. This is a large order. No living person can give me the excitement I got at eight years old when father took me on his knee and in vivid Anglo-Saxon words "popularized" for me the theories of Darwin. He was a walking Book of Knowledge. He was delightful; he loved me, he was my slave.

I want a man like that. And he'd better not fall down, as father did to my undying grief and disillusion, in practical details of living which any moron manages with ease. He must not play the violin while the upper field is waiting to be plowed.

The myth of this man, the urge to find him, has been at once my greatest spur to adventure and achievement and a pest of the first magnitude. His actual non-existence is chronically annoying; but that doesn't prevent my seeking. It pushed me out of my backwoods environment; it sent me traveling, experimenting, studying. It prodded me until I could earn my living. It put me into strikes, an amateur Joan of Arc. It projected me into the Middle West in the campaign which gave Wilson his chance to keep us out of war; it has pinned my hopes on utopias of all kinds. Whenever I find my energies flowing out in a large and embattled way I can, in five minutes of reflection, discover trails which twist and tangle, cross and recross, join at last, and lead back to a tall man with dark-blue, animated eyes, sitting in a smoke-browned New England kitchen, talking passionately, talking, talking....

My sister, a year and a half younger, did not share my adoration of father. She found him, on the contrary, an unendurable bore. She ran away from the conversation that charmed me. She, too, was a precocious child—but her precocity differed from mine. She had no curious hunger for the alphabet, no special affinity for the printed page. But she could run swiftly on sure feet at the age of nine months, and she used with skill the blocks and toys which I had only looked at meditatively. When we were old enough to help about the house, my cakes burned and my jelly would not "jell"; for me the cows refused to yield their milk, and horses, feeling my hands upon the reins, ignored me. But my sister excelled at housekeeping and managed the farm animals. She loved to drive the harrows and horse-rakes. She was famous for fast running and high climbing. But with all her daring and capacity for man's work she is not a feminist. She is a well-adjusted wife and mother, and a leader in Farm Bureau and rural-school activities. There is not an impractical fiber in her make-up. No trace of father is visible in the silent, prudent, capable man she chose for a husband.

Is the modern woman conditioned by what the Freudians call a "father complex"? Do her emotions search for satisfactions that never existed and thus lose their relation to biological processes? Perhaps this is true, and yet—There was mother, a stodgy, quiet woman, not an intellectual, and herself without a scintillating father; mother and her one aberrant quality: a desire for a colorful mate, a disgust with all dull men.

Physically I am almost a replica of mother. Yet I carry in my harassed inwards the conflicts of both my parents. I could, I think, write extraordinary literature—if I did not have to toil on bread-and-butter copy. That is like father. I have mother's liking for security and stability.

I have been married ten years, satisfactorily as marriage goes, to a man a trifle like father. He cares too much about amusing living to be a proper Rotarian and go-getter. Yet he does not measure up to the myth —no man could. However, I have weathered my disappointment; I stand off and look at the situation from the outside, laugh at it, manage it a bit. Only this saves my very agreeable husband from a horrid fate.

I consider our marriage permanent. The realities of marriage have had a tendency to terminate my long quest. In making a tolerable life of sex and friendship, in earning my living, in fighting for the kind of work I want, emergencies have arisen in which it has been necessary to look at impedimenta critically and to modify feelings and habits of dubious worth. So a pioneer crossing a ford might be compelled to throw overboard grandfather's clock—might discover, too, as he watched its ancient form go bumping down the stream that he was glad to be rid of its bulk and its everlasting ticking. My common sense long ago convinced me that my search for a Prince Charming should no longer be conducted with a view to practical results. It is still true, however, that the same old dynamo furnishes the motive power for my actions. As a little girl I worked for good report-cards to draw a friendly glint from father's eye. I would come home from Normal School in my teens and preen before him in my new learning.

After childhood was over and I turned to the business of earning a living and finding a mate, there were years when I scarcely gave my father a thought. But as a young newspaper reporter I dogged the footsteps of intellectual men. I gave tactful publicity to learned professors (providing they were tall), to handsome violinists, to a shrewd corporation lawyer who let me browse in his private library, to a railroad vice-president who poured forth copious language in answer to my questions. Long after it was clear to me that I was only bored by the organization of labor groups I kept on in order to enjoy the conversation and the approval of a certain liberal leader who reminded me of father.

Somewhere I have read of a musical composer who worked best when assailed by the smell of rotten apples, a smell which no doubt evoked an emotional satisfaction of childhood. Before he began the day's work he filled the drawers of his desk with them. In some such way I try before beginning a piece of creative work to talk a bit with some man who is older and presumably wiser than I, whose mind sparkles and who improvises well as he talks.

I am exacting in selecting these fathers. As long as I can believe in the overwhelming superiority of any one of them he casts a spell, and I can put through, after being with him, an enormous quantity of work. But as time goes on the number of such men tends to diminish. At thirty-odd it is hard to find a man who will respond to every question with a cascade of creative talk and who can toss unheard-of systems of philosophy through the air like a juggler's balls. With unfortunate celerity I catch Homer nodding and he is ruined. Often, when younger, I suffered poignant grief when a father toppled; but now I take such catastrophes with philosophy.

I no longer work on movements. My energies are bent on achieving an income which will enable me to write realistic novels. Do I want to do good work for the joy of creative effort, for the satisfaction of putting my life across? I believe I do—yet dimly, as through a vapor, I see the future: my books written, and some very, very great father, Bernard Shaw, Einstein, goodness knows who, coming forward to speak to me kindly and blow off a shower of glittering intellectual sparks—for me, personally.

RUTH PICKERING

Ruth Pickering calls herself "a deflated rebel," but her essay suggests that her rebellion was always ambivalent. Her commitment to feminism seems in many ways to have been a rejection of the traditional female culture epitomized by her powerful grandmother Evans. Before 1920, Ruth Pickering joined Heterodoxy; as a journalist she wrote on the labor movement. After her marriage, however, she made her career out of writing about the kinds of "womanly" cultural interests she had despised as a girl. In the 1920s, she wrote for *The Nation* and *New Republic* on dance, jazz, and modern art. In the 1930s, she became associate editor of *Arts and Decoration*. Pickering speaks for the individualistic "new-style feminist" of the 1920s, declaring that "my feminism is a part of my ego and perhaps nothing more."

A Deflated Rebel

From a rebellious childhood I have settled into a comfortable middle age of marriage, children, a couple of strenuous and pleasantly creative avocations, and a slight tendency to bridle when men deal in generalizations about women—despite the fact that I indulge in generalizations about men. An explanation of my continuously angry soul as a child is as far beyond me as an explanation of my present complacency. But I find an impersonal interest in the conflicts which surrounded us at home, now that they are revealed. They were at the time unmentioned and by an heroic effort almost unnoticed in our upright Quaker household.

Women predominated in the family. We were two grandmothers, father, mother, and three daughters. Grandfather Evans, who left at his death a business which was our life's catastrophe, dominated the family circle to some extent by his grave portrait and by my grandmother's and my mother's adoration of him as a symbol of great competence. Grandfather Haynes, a vague family hero, since he lost his life in an underground railway freeing slaves, was unknown even to my father, born after his death.

Father and mother married about the time of her father's death. Owing to a flight in advertising, his business was willed to his widow and daughter (my mother) in a bankrupt condition. Bankruptcy proceedings would have saved the day, but my Grandmother Evans's proud and stubborn spirit prevented. Therefore, as my father and mother started on their marital career, they assumed the responsibility of paying off an enormous debt, reviving a fading business, supporting two grandmothers, and keeping intact the large house and garden of my mother's mother. We had to move into this house within a few years to save expense. Grandma Evans looked upon this arrangement as an imposition, although her own rigid and upright standards of conduct had made it necessary. But sacrifices were essential. My grandmother's maid must go; our "hired girl" must go. The house was apportioned; the household work divided.

Now for various reasons my father's mother, Grandma Haynes, a good and kindly practicing Quaker, was thoroughly despised by my mother's mother, an intelligent and presumably gentle practicing Quaker. I think Grandma Haynes was considered "common," or perhaps it was her more poverty-stricken past that gained her my other grandmother's antagonism. But the problem of keeping these two eminently sweet old ladies from meeting in the house became another burden upon my father and mother. Grandma Evans would peer down the long hall from the door of her room before stepping out in order to guard against any chance meeting with Grandma Haynes. Should that tragic event occur in spite of every precaution, there would be a quickened tread and an averted head on the part of Grandma Evans and a sad, hurt look of bewilderment on the face of Grandma Haynes. When I witnessed one of these meetings, the gorge rose within me. I was aligned forever with the more humble side of the family—my Grandmother Haynes and her son, my father.

The division of tasks in the household was tragically perverse. Grandma Evans—intellectual, individualist, and undomestic— assumed complete charge of the kitchen, planning and cooking for this entire family which her conscience had imposed upon her. Otherwise her martyrdom would have been insufficient, and we should have been less in the position of irritating and unwelcome guests. Grandma Haynes, who craved hard manual labor for the sake of those she loved, was barred from the kitchen. She was forced to eke out her unsatisfied zeal in devoted care of us—who would have none of it—and in endless knitting. Besides the kitchen Grandma Evans had as her sanctuary the library, with heavy doors eternally drawn together, and her own front bedroom. Neither of these rooms can I ever remember entering, except to sniff their dignity and remoteness. Her quiet superiority and her endless labor were exasperatingly evident; though she never complained or discussed her affairs in our hearing. Utterly dependent on my father and mother, she was yet the unquestioned head of the house, while they were the driven slaves of the business she had refused to allow them to abandon.

Grandma Haynes was more a part of the family. We all, except Grandma Evans, used the office, which English-like was in the house, in the evening as a sitting-room. Here my mother and father worked at the ledgers and typewriter during the day; here an enormous safe bearing my grandfather's name, fondly surrounded by pink painted roses and many flourishes, was a constant reminder of his once prosperous state. The parlor was for piano lessons and parties.

We children were brought up to speak the Quaker tongue out of consideration for our grandmothers, and the Quaker tongue in a thoroughly un-Quaker community in the mouths of three fairly unrefined little brats often expresses itself in such demure remarks as "Damn thee. I'm just as tough as thee is."

But to Grandma Evans was due more than mere respect. Virtue in our family consisted in helping her with the dishes and household chores. Wickedness was to refuse dishwashing and play with the undesirable family next door, whom Grandma Evans despised but whom my father and Grandma Haynes could see no reason for disdaining, poor and uneducated though they were. My elder sister chose the good; I chose the evil; my younger sister remained neutral. I chose the side of no work and free associations. I rebelled against the quiet superiority which lent a fictitious dignity to tiresome tasks and poured silent contempt on the gentle head of Grandma Haynes. Although the antagonism between them was unspoken and unacknowledged, I sided passionately with the under-grandmother and rejected all the standards set up by Grandma Evans. Perhaps I yearned secretly for her approval, but could not stoop to win it. Certainly I did not. I went my way, angry and resentful. I sought out the toughest companions of the neighborhood. I played with boys winter and summer, whose bravado, being normal, seemed of a far less glorious nature than my own. They were no better and no worse than I at the game of tip-cat under the lamplight on the corner of a spring evening. Boys were slightly more stupid in school, but occasionally better at games. Though I tried football, it bored me and I freely granted superiority on that field if they claimed it. I felt magnificently glorified in being a girl—a girl who could do anything she wanted to. I also felt proud of my democratic ways. I played with and liked the most "undesirable" children I could find, just as at home I associated with and adored the grandmother who I knew was looked down upon. Having to do dishes and run errands was an injustice; and so was our everlasting economy and poverty. I was in a state of continual rebellion.

Since we were brought up with economic handicaps, it had been taken for granted by us all that once out of college the efforts of our father and mother were finished as far as we were concerned. We had to earn our own living; no feminist faith was necessary. Since the work of supporting the family had been done as much by my mother as by my father, there was nothing to indicate that we should not be as capable of earning money as any son would have been. I can remember no suggestion in the minds of any of us of sex inferiority, male or female. Both my father and mother believed in and worked for woman suffrage. There was no preaching to us of woman's duty being thus and so. Certainly we were not brought up to be charming; our clothes were grotesque, expressing my mother's latent color sense, if they expressed anything at all.

Later on, in college, I became imbued with sufficient formulism to feel that it was up to me to prove that women were as capable as men in the world's achievements. But owing to a natural dislike of hard work, still heavy upon me from childhood, I was soon able to prove to my own satisfaction that no important task had to be done by me as a woman, since other women were covering themselves with glory in every field of effort. That let me out personally. Inwardly, I looked upon earning my living primarily as a chance for further adventure, for experience and amusement, and gained my objective with scant satisfaction to my employers. I worked in factories; briefly I held a position as secretary; I went in for newspaper and magazine work. I enjoyed my various jobs for the personal contacts they involved, for their variety and occasional excitement. I disliked them for their drudgery—the reminiscent flavor of duty and dishwashing.

In the early days of my marriage the formulas of feminism pestered me because I allowed my husband to support me. But since I had used my economic independence previously as a means to adventure, and the immediate adventure of my life was the entirely unforeseen one of adjusting to intimacy and conflict in marriage, I found it easy to still the accusing voice which pointed out that principles were at stake. Besides which, having found that most of my principles were generated out of perversity, it became necessary as I grew older either to cast rigid rules of conduct out altogether or to invent them as the situation arose or to remold new ones out of a more adult attitude. My feminism is a part of my ego and perhaps nothing more. I like myself—and I am a woman. Therefore, I naturally resent injustice on the basis of sex.

As an individual I want, and have found, an opportunity to do what interests me—inside my home and outside as well. My deficiencies and my capacities are my own—not those of my sex. Having come from under the pressure to perform imposed tasks I have gained both freedom and eagerness in the work I do. Since I no longer have to work, I am no longer lazy; since I am not disapproved of, I am not angry. I have traded my sense of exhilarating defiance (shall we call it feminism?) for an assurance of free and unimpeded self-expression (or shall we call that feminism?). In other words, I have grown up.

GENEVIEVE TAGGARD

Like several other women in the *Nation* series, the poet Genevieve Taggard (1894-1948) used her essay to explore some of her feelings about her mother, and through those feelings to analyze female experience in America. While she writes about her mother as the antagonist whose fundamentalist religion, authoritarianism, and domestic tyranny she had plotted to escape, Taggard nonetheless recognizes her kinship to her mother and their mutual connection to an American tradition of strong, often thwarted, women pioneers.

Taggard's parents were missionaries who ran a church school in Hawaii. Growing up in an interracial, uninhibited society gave her a radical perspective on the values of small-town America and helped her to resist the pressures to conform which the family encountered on two unhappy returns to their native Washington. Brilliant, ambitious, and disciplined, she taught herself enough Latin to pass the entrance exams to Berkeley, graduating in 1919. Her first nationally published poem appeared in *Harper's* the same year.

A lifelong socialist, Taggard wrote for Max Eastman's *Liberator* and served, with her first husband, Robert Wolf, as contributing editor to the *New Masses*. Never an activist in women's causes, she was fascinated with women of determination and endurance and often celebrated them in her writing. In 1930, she published a critical biography of Emily Dickinson. Taggard's introduction to her own *Collected Poems 1918-1938* expressed her wish to transcend the category of "poetess" to which critics had frequently assigned her, along with her contemporaries Edna St. Vincent Millay and Sara Teasdale:

Many poems in this collection are about the experiences of women. I hope these express all types of candid and sturdy women.....All those who try to live richly and intelligently. I have refused to write out of a decorative impulse, because I conceive it to be the dead end of much feminine talent. A kind of literary needlework. I think the later poems and some of the early ones hold a wider consciousness than that colored by the feminine half of the race. I hope they are not written by a poetess, but by a poet. I think, I hope, I have written poetry that relates to general experience and the realities of the time.

In the 1930s, Taggard held a number of teaching jobs at women's colleges including Bennington and Sarah Lawrence. Her marriage to Robert Wolf ended in 1934, and the next year she married Kenneth Durant, American director for the Soviet news agency Tass.

Taggard's feminism comes from her need for self-sufficiency as an artist and as a worker. In her own family, she had seen her mother's strength turn sour in a marriage to a passive man, and she wondered whether it could ever be possible for equals to live in equilibrium together. What makes her "modern" is her conviction that "it is better to work hard than to be married hard." She defines her priorities in terms of self-development, not in terms of a difficult, challenging, time-and-energy-consuming relationship.

Poet Out of Pioneer

My mother and father were the two most remarkable young people in a very small Western town: my mother, a pioneer extravert, a hard-working, high-handed, generous, and handsome girl. She never set limits to what she could do. She believed in miracles made by her own hands. When my father came, she was in rebellion against small-town sterility, determined to go to college and become, not a raw country girl with the limit of grammar-school learning but a cultured Christian gentlewoman, who could paint, sing, write, and testify to God's glory. My father had come West from Missouri for his health. He looked like

Abraham Lincoln, but delicate and Quixotic. My mother's strength fascinated him and, I suppose, scared him to death. Church and school linked them—he, the principal of the grammar school; in a crude community, a man of learning (six months in a church college); the superintendent of the Sunday school and leader of Christian Endeavor. She was his first-grade teacher and a very good one. Not for nothing had she been mother to eleven brothers and sisters on the old ranch. She ran her schoolroom with an energy that was electric. Children were happy with her. She furnished them a firm foundation.

My father, of course, felt the charge of vitality. They married and for two years lived in a state of enforced chastity, I suppose, determined to save money and go to college. They saved $2,000 and were departing for a higher life when my uncle, my father's brother, came penniless from the East and married a shrew. My father loved my uncle with an unnatural simplicity. Brother John and the shrew wanted the two thousand to buy an apple-farm. My mother saw an older love in my tender father about to swamp her ambitions. In this emotional tangle I was conceived and it was I, finally, not my father or my uncle, who defeated my mother. The money went of course to John, college plunged into inaccessibility, and my mother was in the usual trap and, I am sure, as bitter as any modern woman about it.

Suddenly came a chance to go to a tropic country—another way out. Romanticists they both were, although they called themselves missionaries. And so when I was still a baby my mother gave the rest of her possessions to my uncle, packed up me and her baffled desires, and set off with her Shelleyesque husband to the heathen. The story is a complicated one; I shall follow only the trends of the two temperaments. My mother, with ultimately three children and a passive husband, still had her old ambitions in this new land. But with us she did not encourage the freedom she gave her little school-children. At home she was a major domo. The family became a highly efficient organization—it had to be, when she gave most of her day to teaching. Although she took care of us all, there was never any ease or leisure; we were not permitted happiness. In the public school and the missionary chapel these two labored, giving their crowded time free for Jesus. My father was the principal, a flexible glove on my mother's strong, stubby hand. She was still his "primary" teacher, his wife, cook, housekeeper, refuge, and intelligence. And so complete was her domination over her man that she expected to mold and use me as she had used him.

But I, of course, began before I can remember silently and consistently to oppose her; to defend my father and to rebel at her steamroller tactics. I was lonely and excitable. Fairy-tales were denied me—no reading but the Bible—so I made Bible stores into fairy-tales and she found me very difficult about them. She believed in authority. I would not submit to it. She drove me to music lessons and housework—all done to the moral precept: *there is only one right way.* I should have been a musician or a composer; but she blocked the path, hemmed in with her vigilance all creation. Music, made hideous in the guise of duty, I abandoned and took another way out—with words, where no one could give me orders. I dreamed and made fantasies, and soon I lied habitually, to escape her, and went underground in all my desires. I was my father again, but a girl this time, and enough like herself to match her mettle. I had a good childhood in spite of the fact that we lived in a state of nervous tension at home and, as missionaries and school people, in a superior and controlled fashion in public, upholding the just, the good, the true. That was easy because we had the advantage of our less educated native neighbors. My father, as the years went by, became a vague sort of scientist, fleeing away from my mother's pressure. She, passionate and unfulfilled, lived in her three children.

Her objective was this cultural life she had never reached herself, and toward it our faces were always directed. But there was a division in my mother's own mind which she had never faced. Our religion was the religion of the small town, based on a fear of the big world, on a fear of the rational, the progressive, and the huge bugaboo of "Darwinism" and Higher Criticism. And yet however my mother fought against the liberal Congregationalists and the damned Unitarians, and however fanatical was her matter-of-fact mysticism, she wanted her children to live in that intellectual world and, I suppose, to solve, in a Christian fashion, its problem for her.

Twice my father collapsed and was told to his immense relief that he had tuberculosis and that he need no longer inhabit our world. His ailment was undoubtedly psychological. Twice we starved, and adored our mother for her gorgeous strength, and pitied and averted our faces from our father. And then the old theme reentered.

My mother demanded of my now wealthy Uncle John the $2,000 that had made him a comfortable apple-grower, and had kept her in bondage. We lived on canned salmon and rice and wild tomatoes for several months, in a shack where the tropic rains poured on our beds;

and John wrote evasively with no inclosures. My father loved him still and would do nothing about it. My mother went as nearly insane with rage as she could permit herself, but only on Saturday mornings, when she could safely compute compound interest on an outlawed loan. The story spins out and out. We returned to the small town in an attempt to collect the two thousand, after a letter from my uncle offering us an old farmhouse near him. There, used as my uncle's hired help and wearing his family's cast-off clothing, we integrated ourselves into the single struggle to exist—without him. At length we returned to our tropics, penniless still, but to decent poverty and our own way of life. And my mother and father took up their teaching where they had begun fourteen years before, in a three-room school on a sugar plantation. This was a little too ironic for my frail father who had just managed to complete before his return to the States a twelve-room modern school for his beloved natives. He fell ill again and again we existed—I teaching in his place to get the $25 a month allotted a substitute.

I was ready for college. On two hundred borrowed dollars we came to a Western university town and there as servants in a boarding-house began again the struggle that included our whole story.

Am I the Christian gentlewoman my mother slaved to make me? No indeed. I am a poet, a wine-bibber, a radical; a non-churchgoer who will no longer sing in the choir or lead prayer-meeting with a testimonial. (Although I will write anonymous confessions for *The Nation*.) That is her story—and her second defeat. She thinks I owed her a Christian gentlewoman, for all she did for me. We quarrel. After I escaped, she snapped shut the iron trap around my brother and sister. That is their story. I do not know if they will ever be free of her. She keeps Eddie Guest on the parlor table beside the books I have written—a silent protest against me. She is not pleased.

I cannot pretend to be entirely frank in telling the story that results from this story; or to apply to it any such perspective. Let my daughter tell it later on. She will see outlines I cannot.

I think I have not been as wasted as my mother was—or as wasteful. I have made worse mistakes, which might have been more fatal than hers and yet have not been, at least for me. My chief improvement on her past was the man I chose to marry. I did not want a one-way street of a marriage, like hers. I married a poet and novelist, gifted and difficult, who refused defeat as often as I did. Hard as it is to live with an equal, it is at least not degrading. We have starved, too;

struggled as hard as ever my folks did. But the struggle has not been empty; I have no grudges. Intellectually as well as emotionally my husband had as much to give that was new and strange as I had. In marriage I learned, rather tardily, the profound truth that contradicts Jesus when he said, "Bear ye one another's burdens." I am a better person when I bear my own burdens. I am happiest with people who can bear their own, too. I remember my mother's weariness and contempt for a man who could never take up her challenges. Seven years with a real person is better than her thirty with a helpless, newspaper-reading gentleman.

The pioneer woman was a dynamo—and her man nearly always ran out on her. From the bitterness in such women many of us were born. Where was her mate? Did she destroy him? Did he hate her for her strength? Was he weaker because she was strong? Where is the equilibrium, anyway? I do not know, for sure, although I spend much time wondering.

Marriage is the only profound human experience; all other human angles are its mere rehearsal. Like every one else I have wanted it. And yet having it, it is not all I want. It is more often, I think, a final experience than a way of life. But I am a poet—love and mutual living are not nearly enough. It is better to work hard than to be married hard. If, at the beginning of middle age, we have not learned some of the perils of the soul, in this double-selved life, we are pure fools. Self-sufficiency is a myth, of course, but after thirty, if one is a serious-minded egoist (i.e., artist) it becomes more and more necessary. And I think it can be approximated.

Lucinda Matlock, in the "Spoon River Anthology," says:

> We were married and lived together for seventy years,
> Enjoying, working, raising the twelve children,
> Eight of whom we lost,
> Ere I had reached the age of sixty.
> I spun, I wove, I kept the house, I nursed the sick,
> Rambling over the fields where sang the larks,
> And by Spoon River gathering many a shell,
> And many a flower and medicinal weed,
> Shouting to the wooded hills, singing to the green valleys.
> At ninety-six I had lived long enough, that is all,
> And passed to a sweet repose.
> What is this I hear of sorrow and weariness,

Anger, discontent, and drooping hopes?
Degenerate sons and daughters,
Life is too strong for you—
It takes life to love Life.

My mother was not this woman, nor am I, but we are both some way kin to her.

7

LORINE LIVINGSTON PRUETTE

Lorine Pruette (1876-) was one of the young women social scientists of the 1920s who adapted modernism into a feminist vision. Born in Tennessee, Pruette went from college to graduate work at Clark University, where she studied with the psychologist G. Stanley Hall. Her biography, *G. Stanley Hall* (1926), expresses her intense admiration for this influential professor. Her childhood experience with a father who could do nothing except "ride a horse and boss the Negroes," gave her a strong conviction that "women had all the children, men had all the fun, and men were pretty awful anyway." But her experience at Clark and her exposure to the work of Havelock Ellis, Freud, and Jung changed her attitudes towards men and marriage.

At Clark, Pruette met Douglas Henry Fryer, another graduate student. In 1920, they were married and moved to New York, where he became an instructor in the Columbia psychology department and she enrolled in the Ph.D. program, receiving her degree in 1924. For several years she adapted to his career, following him as he changed jobs. Pruette found a variety of positions outside academia, working as a consultant to Macy's and to several New York hospitals, and writing for *The New York Times, The New York Herald Tribune, The Saturday Evening Post,* and many professional journals. Her thesis, *Women and Leisure,* was published in 1924. Despite her positive comments about her marriage in the *Nation* essay, there were many strains. Recalling this period of her life, in 1975, she wrote:

After a few years we wanted to go to Europe for his sabbatical. About that time Guggenheim had started in with fellowships. I had had two books published to good reviews. It seemed reasonable to expect a fellowship. I had a couple of famous sponsors. He decided to apply also. I saw no reason but thought it his own business. No answer for either of us. Next year in Spain...secy. of Guggenheim said they had a policy—no fellowships for wife unless husband also got one. So male chauvinism wrecked my plans.

He always applied for anything which seemed suitable for me. Was he competing with me? I suspect so. He had told me he knew I was smarter than he was. I was a better writer. If I were sitting in my room, reading a magazine, he would come in, say, well dear, you're not doing anything—will you rewrite this article for me? He thought reading was not doing anything! I did not agree.

They were divorced, and in 1932, Pruette married John Woodbridge Herring, a New York educational theorist; this marriage too ended, in two years. When she writes, in "Why Women Fail," that most husbands do not want their wives to have too much success, Pruette seems to be speaking from personal experience. Much of her work deals with the problems of integrating women's personal and public lives. In 1929, she advocated part-time jobs as a way of allowing married women to maintain some economic independence and work experience ("The Married Woman and the Part-time Job," *Annals of the American Academy of Political and Social Science*). An active and energetic economist through the war, Lorine Pruette now lives in a rest home in Tennessee; she has kept up with the Women's Liberation Movement, and her sense of humor and audacity are undiminished.

The Evolution of Disenchantment

As one of those awful Southerners in the North, I shall have to begin with the Civil War. Of course there were earlier wars in the family annals, but I do not feel so personally responsible for them. Grandpapa A gave some money to the Confederate Army and stayed at home to look after his possessions, consequently came out of the war pretty well off, continued to beget daughters, and in his old age was rewarded by the appearance of a son who was to be my father. When I was very young I thought it a terrible disgrace that Grandpapa A had not gone to fight the Yankees; now I regard his perspicacity somewhat differently. Grandpapa B was a hero and went to war (it now appears that he went reluctantly but it was a long time before I knew this), ruined his health, came home to dire poverty, begat a number of children, and died with suspicious readiness. My mother was his oldest daughter.

Papa was a good-looking young man, trained to do nothing, who drove a fast horse and was supposed to have money. Mama was such a good girl that when a man once told her she had a pretty foot she blushed and wondered if she should feel insulted. The last cent of her inheritance from her grandfather had paid for her college diploma. She had taught school for a year and been sick most of the time; her mother told her to get married. So the city girl drove back of that fast-stepping horse to her country home; all the male relatives of the groom got drunk at the wedding supper and I was born as speedily as possible, not as an accident but as the natural consequence of ignorance. The physician was papa's brother-in-law and an autocrat; he believed that women should suffer in childbirth and refused to administer chloroform during the process. The parents were twenty-two years old, papa startled but inclined to strut, mama consumed with bitterness and terrified of having another baby, all three of us surrounded by a family organization tighter than a band of steel. It was determined that the only son must stay on the land, in spite of the fact that all other decent families had moved away and tenant-farmers were all around beginning their devastating efforts.

There was not a thing papa knew how to do except ride a horse and boss the Negroes about the crops. It developed, too, that after Grandpapa B had given each of his girls a good wedding and two thousand dollars there was not much left except the two farms. So we lived with the bluegrass hills and the rattlesnakes, the mocking birds and the darkies, my mother in a terror of childbirth and I in a loneliness not greatly mitigated by the contempt in which I was taught to hold all other children in the vicinity. I could play with the Negro children, who knew they were my inferiors, but I could not play with the white children, who might want to dispute this. The Negroes, too, taught me to despise the white tenants as trash, so it was not hard for me to perceive that my family was the most remarkable in the world. But those lonely, bitter years were a crime against childhood; I shall not ever lose their scar. There was always plenty of money for newfangled and useless machinery, never any for books; the small girl read Shakespeare and the poems of Edgar Poe; she thrilled over the composition books in which her mother had written college themes; she determined to be a writer.

Before I was six I knew that men could do something terrible to women, and I flamed with the injustice of it. I ached with the longing to make it up to my mother and I braced myself against the dining table to tell my father that I hated him, then fled in terror before his threatened vengeance. That ache and that hatred continued until I was myself out of college, and there have been many nights when I have stayed awake planning desperately how to make a great deal of money and take my mother away from my father. Now I know that she would not have gone; now I know that there were compensations which she never allowed me to suspect, and that there was never any reason for things to be half as bad as I thought them. But the scar remains.

When I was seven we moved to the city. My mother's family, more prosperous now, made a place for my father which he took on sufferance, always with the threat that he would soon be going back to the country. Once we did go back and I hated him worse than ever, but we did not stay long. In business my father has always been the kind of man who comes out of a trade poorer than he went in; he has the need to be generous and lordly and superior to money; he wants to give things away in order to assure himself that he is of some importance in the world. When I was seven there was also a little brother to relieve me of some of the injurious strain of my mother's devotion.

My two grandmothers must not be omitted. They were very different, except that both were proud as peacocks. Neither had any just cause for pride, but that was the way they had been brought up. They outlived their husbands many years and continued to dominate the families. My mother's mother was the daughter of a country doctor who roused the ridicule of his patients by the education he insisted on giving his girls. Perhaps it is from him I get my feministic strain. I doubt if either grandmother felt it was any particular hardship to be a woman; they were both vigorous, able women, capable of getting a great deal of enjoyment out of life. They took, as I remember, a rather tolerant and somewhat amused attitude toward the men of the family; it was my mother's mother who used to check me up when I said bitter things against men or specifically against my father.

By the time I reached my teens I had a well-developed dogma on the world's injustice toward women because they could not have everything they wanted, on nature's injustice toward women because they have to bear the children, and a lack of interest in God because he was a man. A lady god would have roused my soul's devotion. It is true I did get religion when I was about twelve, being then jointly in love with the minister and the minister's daughter. I spent an afternoon kneeling at the altar and tried to feel uplifted, but without great success; told my Sunday-school teacher of the visions I had and despised her for appearing to believe me. Then at fifteen I fell in love with a language teacher who was an atheist and lost my religion. Thereafter I had only one religion, a sort of perverse feminism, based on the convictions that women had all the children, men had all the fun, and men were pretty awful anyhow. I was still determined to have a career as much like a man's as possible. And no babies. And no matrimony.

Mama said she wanted me to have three good offers and to refuse three. She wanted me to be a glorified old maid, doing the things she might have done. I decided I would get married when I was thirty, in order to have tried everything, and then I advanced the date by six years to get rid of the argument: to be or not to be. It seemed to me it might be pleasant to have something settled, even though the settlement itself was bad. Then I had begun to suspect that marriage could not possibly be as bad as I had thought it. And I had met some Northern men who seemed to think women might be treated more or less as adults and who were willing to assume some of the responsibilities for the more boresome side of domestic life. I had lived too long in a family of men who in times of distress remained pleasantly incapable of making a cup of coffee; I do not believe I could have married a Southerner, and if I had I am sure I would have murdered him the first time he asked for his slippers or the evening paper. So I married a Yankee and found marriage not so bad as it might have been, nor yet so good. At any rate I got that cause of conflict more or less settled. My husband is interested in my work and I am interested in his; at a pinch we substitute for each other, though this is growing more difficult as we grow older and our interests become more specialized. He is eager for me to develop as far as I can, and he has few theories about woman's position, or man's. We keep house casually and travel a good deal. My own diathesis is against anything that is fixed. We have no children and thus my mother's old terrors are laid for me.

The war swung me out of college into a totally unexpected job. Since then I have dabbled a bit in college teaching and a bit in research. Over the college teaching I was discouraged because, while I liked the students, I found it rather dull ladling out platitudes to the indifferent adolescent, and I could see no prospect of working into graduate teaching. Women do not, as yet, get much chance at this cream of the teaching profession. In research I shall always be interested, though here, too, I am hampered by my attitude of disenchantment. I can never quite accept the finality of a statistical formula, and the errors which are constantly being demonstrated in the work of even the best scientists make me a little dubious about branding any conclusion as the Truth in capital letters. I can still get mad when I see an obvious case of discrimination against women, but in general all my old feministic revolt has been transferred from men to the conditions of human existence. There is nothing any of us can do about these conditions which does not seem to me futile, so my only test for different activities is the pleasure to be derived from them.

Thus I have at a comparatively early age lost all my motivating faiths, faith in the righteous cause of women, faith in the recreating powers of science, faith in the ennobling possibilities of education. This is indeed a very sad state. Worse, I have become that futile creature, a writer. I had rather make small black marks on paper than go through any experience I can name. The sensory pleasures have pretty largely ceased to be; I can sit here in my quiet study and desire to desire something, something to touch or taste or see or hear, but the desire does not come. If I were building a Utopia, I would take away our memories, so we would start fresh every day, and then I would endow each of us with strong, lusty desires, and I would give us strong, eager feet with which to run swiftly and determinedly after our desires. I would leave principles out of my Utopia, even feminism; in place of principles I would give us all a magnificent and flaming audacity.

KATE L. GREGG

"Who cares what the psychoanalyst will say?" Kate Gregg writes defiantly. As a woman who had overcome tremendous obstacles to earn a Ph.D. in English from the University of Wisconsin in 1916, Gregg was proud of her accomplishments and satisfied with her life. Having seen in her own family the exploitation of a woman tied to an irresponsible and unsuccessful man, she refused three proposals of marriage. Instead she pursued her academic career. Gregg's self-acceptance, her still-intense anger on her mother's behalf, her insistence on economic independence, and her refusal to compromise irked one of the psychologists, Joseph Collins, who referred to her as "the celibate": "Despite the celibate's self-complacency, her life is incomplete. To pretend that she has handled the marriage-problem by avoiding love in or out of marriage is fatuous." Yet from a less orthodox, less marriage-bound perspective, Gregg's life is an example of the way many kinds of love can enrich a woman's life; how love diffused through family and work can provide the satisfactions that traditionally are expected from a more intense two-person relationship. The way to freedom that she advocates is not lovelessness, but "the need for economic independence for women as an honorable and self-respecting basis for love and marriage."

One Way to Freedom

A little girl of six or seven, clinging to a rickety picket fence and listening, still and intent as if she listened with her whole body instead of with ears alone. Coming? Yes, of course, he was coming. Mama was too anxious. There—a little hint of sound again. The murmur of wagon wheels maybe on the hill beyond the second slough. Hope shot through her young heart. The wagon would rumble loudly and certainly when it came to the corduroy at the foot of the hill. Breathless she waited as if all life depended on her hearing. Her young mother came silently from the kitchen door and joined her.

"Yes, I thought I heard something, mama. Listen. Maybe now he will pass over the bridge at the slough." But even hope could hear nothing more definite than the wind in the fir trees at the edge of the little prairie. So they listened, mother and daughter both, in the spring, summer, autumn, winter twilight. Listened every time he went to town, and heartsick knew they hoped in vain.

It was always the same story. Oats to be ground into chop, hogs to be marketed, grain to be hauled to the warehouse, winter supplies to be bought, taxes to be paid, interest to be met—each time there was the sickening uncertainty as to whether he would come home cheery and happy when he ought to come or whether mother would have to do the farm chores, four little children left in the house alone with the fires, or trailing her skirts as she milked cows, fed horses, cleaned stables; and he, the father, would come a week later, hang-dog and ashamed because he had succumbed to another periodical spree, and had spent not only himself but all the family income as well, derived from hogs, grain, hay, and dedicated to winter groceries, taxes, or interest.

Always there were children, four then, and more as the years went by until mother had given birth to eight. To the despair that grew in her in consequence of the repeated sprees was added the deadly certainty of another child inevitably near. When the fourth child was born, father disappeared the day after to be gone a week or ten days, and I can remember yet mother's explanation to hired girl and midwife —it was always both in one for us—that Mr. ——— had been called away on business. Would he be home for dinner today? Day after day she could not say, she did not know. When we had moved for the third time, far away this time from anybody who had ever known us before, her hour for a sixth deliverance close at hand, and he, the father, gone again to exercise his individual liberty, I saw her one night get out the family revolver, oil it, load it, and place it under her pillow. When, white and sick from foreboding, I ventured to ask, "Why that?" she answered, "If it comes upon me when he is gone and nobody here to take care of me, I am through, that's all." Child of thirteen that I was then, I argued the silliness of that, and urged my own capacity to do as much as he could do.

This was the man I then knew best. Good natured, easy-going, loving my mother and his children in his own way, but selfish and irresponsible, *wicked* it seemed to me then, in his capacity for inflicting suffering and humiliation. Now after thirty years, and he ten years gone forever, I cannot find much easier words. As the oldest of the children and the nearest to my mother, I experienced her anxieties as if they had been my own, and because I loved her I hated the poverty, shame, and endless child-bearing forced upon her. I cannot remember a time when I did not look upon my father with reproach and often with feelings not to be described by so mild a term.

My mother's dominant passion for me, through these years, and for the five other daughters who came in the course of time, was a desire for our education, that we might fit ourselves for work and for salaries that would make us independent of marriage, or if we did elect it, able to leave it if it were unsatisfactory. She herself had been tied and fettered once for all because she had married at seventeen. An old-fashioned father had refused her the privilege of either going to school or learning a trade, and in marriage which had seemed to offer a way out she had found herself more helpless than ever on account of the never-ending succession of babies. I realize now that mother in her insistence on our schooling was preaching the economic independence of women, though of that as such I am sure she had never heard. She preached it day after day with a singleness of aim and an earnestness that brought to pass what she desired even though the handicaps were well-nigh insurmountable. Education of her daughters every day in the school term, every school term through the years was not to be achieved without domestic battles won only by intensity of purpose and a desire to protect her own. Mother was proud that I never missed school on wash-days, cleaning days, or even when another new baby incapacitated her for a week or two. School for her children was a religion to this mother, and to one end—that we might be free.

She had, of course, educational ideals for her sons, but these were early frustrated by my father's insistence that no mere woman could ever know as much about the desirable education of a male child as a man, with the result that the boys left school in the eighth grade to learn the trade of their father. The younger had a flair for drawing, painting, mathematics, and might have turned into a creditable architect, but he learned to handle the hock and trowel instead. As I look back I realize that a part of father's reluctance to have the boys remain at school was fear lest they be educated into disapproval of himself and his ideal of a man's life.

A great part of the subjection of woman in our family resulted from mother's complete separation from purse-strings. When we lived on the farm, she would earn eight or ten dollars in the course of a year through meals and beds furnished to farmers from the upper country who made our house their stopping-place as they came and went getting in their winter supplies. Yet even getting this much depended on two contingencies. If father was in town engaged in the usual preoccupation, she got the money; or if, he being on the farm, the lodger paid the reckoning into her own hand. Otherwise she lost it entirely. Mother never asked for money for herself, probably because she felt too much humiliated in the asking, but as her girls grew up and needed cash upon occasion, she did it for them. When I had reached high-school and later normal-school age and I needed a dollar a month to pay for my toll ticket across the interstate bridge, she and I alike dreaded the monthly ordeal of getting that dollar. As the time drew near we watched closely for the auspicious occasion that would make reproach least likely. The best time of all was on Saturday night just after supper, when father would be handing out ten dollar bills to the boys "to have a good time."

"Give Cora a dollar, too, daddy. She needs it for toll."

"What? Again?" and the smile of Jove benevolent faded into narrow-eyed suspicion.

As soon as I could attain to the educational distinction of a two years' certificate from the normal school, mother's dream for her eldest was realized, the toll battles were forgotten—one woman at last was free. Eighteen and free. Free to do as I wished with my own.

There were differences between my father and me as to what constituted my own. Through a good many years he suffered from my inability to see that I ought to turn my monthly pay checks over to him; and my silly way of hoarding money for more education gave him acute distress. I remember that when I left for the university, $750 cash in hand—the result of three years' teaching—he sulked in the barn-yard and refused to say goodby. He was indignant to see me throwing away my money. But three years later when I returned I was astonished to know that he was proud that I had graduated and indeed was giving himself some credit for this higher education in the family.

Once the two-year certificate had freed me, not even love's young dream could rob me of wariness. The most desirable youth in the world, in a boy and girl affair, pleaded the blessedness that would ensue if we would but take the reins in our hands and the bits in our teeth (two separate arguments), but realist that I had to be I argued the necessity for his finishing college and getting himself established before we took any fatal steps. And the worst pitfall of all was safely avoided. The most desirable youth in the world was a no-account college student and a philanderer as well, and that was the end of him as an argument. Years afterward I met him again. He had become a second-rate bookkeeper, his wife had had seven children in as many years, of whom only two survived, and every pay-day he handed his salary over to a broker to be gambled on the stock exchange or he lost it in backroom crap games. The home was mortgaged and the wife was sticking it out until the children should be up from under her feet. He was still philandering.

Other men have come my way. One planned a house for me and insisted on a nice big kitchen. That was the end of him. Another dear kind soul with whom I thought I could live rapturously could not build a fire on a camping trip and fancied always when he was lost that the Pacific Ocean must be in the east. The psychoanalyst will say—but who cares what the psychoanalyst will say? I know myself that if I had done otherwise in any one of these three marriage opportunities I would have been a fool.

Having learned my lesson complete and being a creature with a sense of responsibility to womanhood, I have passed on the lesson as best I could. A good many years of my life have gone into helping mother pass it on to my father's other daughters, and being engaged in rearing his family I have felt less the lack of one of my own. All of my sisters have achieved something more than the usual education; some are teachers, some are business women, and any of the three who being married may find in marriage too many fetters has power and ability to strike the irons away. They have, in other words, freedom in their souls.

To confirm the fear of the good souls who tremble for the human race and see it tottering to total extinction as female educationists ply their guile upon the artless young, I might as well now confess that the thirties found me with a doctor's degree, and the forties with a full professorship, in which I enjoy unlimited scope for preaching to men and women alike the need for economic independence of women as an honorable and self-respecting basis for love and marriage. One can hardly hope that lesson is ever learned complete. Perhaps the tranquil, peaceful, rich life I live is more of an argument than any words I shall ever say.

MARY HUNTER AUSTIN

Mary Austin (1868-1934), a novelist, playwright, and folklorist, was probably the most celebrated woman in the *Nation* group. She had achieved critical successes with her novels, especially *A Woman of Genius* (1912) and *No. 26 Jayne Street* (1920); and with her plays, poems, and essays about the Indians of the Southwest. She knew most of the famous writers and artists of the period, from the California group including Jack London and Ina Coolbrith; to Diego Rivera and Mabel Dodge Luhan in Mexico; and H.G. Wells, May Sinclair, and W.B. Yeats in Europe. A lifelong feminist, as a child she had seen Susan B. Anthony, Frances Willard, and Anna Howard Shaw; in New York she knew Emma Goldman, Elizabeth Gurley Flynn, and Margaret Sanger. Austin's autobiography, *Earth Horizon* (1932), is a fascinating account, not only of her own life, but also of the temperance movement, of the difficulties of women settling in the West at the turn of the century, and especially of her mother, Susan Hunter, a complex and tragic woman. Austin's obsession with her mother, who had rejected her repeatedly and yet who loved her and in some ways influenced her, is apparent in her *Nation* piece.

Although she insists that she no longer resents or blames her mother, Austin's sorrow and bitterness permeate her essay.

Austin's life is a testimonial to the tragedies of "enforced maternity" and the double sexual standard. She herself was an unwanted child, born at a time when her mother, who had lost two previous infants, was caring for a semi-invalided husband and a one-year-old son showing signs of some kind of hereditary disease. Throughout her childhood, Austin felt an instinctive sympathy with women's suffering: with the financial struggles of her widowed mother, with the humiliation of the wives of alcoholic and abusive men, and with the unloved and neglected women in the community. In *Earth Horizon* she tells of slapping a man who cursed his wife while she was in labor, an act which for once won her her mother's respect.

Yet her own marriage, to Stafford Wallace Austin in 1891, "failed in almost every particular from which her girlish expectation had been educated." Wallace Austin was irresponsible and constantly in debt; during her pregnancy she worked as a boardinghouse cook to support them both. The birth of their daughter Ruth in 1892 was a disaster from which Mary never recovered. Weak from her labor, and from bad and indifferent medical care, she had to contend with an infant who was constantly sick. Gradually she realized that the child was hopelessly retarded, and, as she hints but never can bring herself to say, that her husband was the carrier of hereditary venereal infection. Neither family would confront the reality of the situation; Mrs. Hunter refused to see the child and told Mary, "I don't know what you've done, daughter, to have such a judgment upon you." Ruth was placed in an institution, where she died in 1918. Austin left her husband in 1907, obtaining a final divorce in 1914.

Austin's analysis of women's "fear of not being liked," though it comes grimly from her own experience, is an important contribution to 1920s feminist theory. Yet her life as a "Woman Alone," showing the high price of emotional independence, was not likely to appeal to the younger generation she so ardently wished to reach.

Woman Alone

The founder of my mother's family came across with Lafayette and married a Massachusetts farmer's daughter with a tradition of Indian blood. By successive removals the family pioneered into Pennsylvania, the Ohio Valley, and the prairies of Illinois. There, in 1861, my mother married a young Englishman who had just won his captaincy in the first three months of the Civil War. A few years after the close of the war I was born as the third of six children. My mother's people were mostly farming folk, though my father was admitted to the bar; he died when I was about ten, of a long-drawn-out war disability. None of the family attained any distinction beyond that of being—the men, good fighters, and the women, notable housewives, rather more forceful and inventive than the men. To account for myself, who turned out to be that blackest of black sheep to a Middle Western family, a radical-minded literary artist, I can record only that my grandfather played the flute and that a member of the French collateral branch was distinguished as a physicist and chemist.

I scarcely know why my being a radical should have proved such a cross to the rest of the family, since they were themselves shouting Methodists, black Abolitionists—my grandfather was known to have entertained Negroes at his table—and my mother a suffragist and an ardent member of the W.C.T.U., which at that time represented the most advanced social thinking among women, saving itself from ostracism only by remaining well within the orthodox religions and confining its activities to moral crusades. There were also "purity leagues" for achieving a single standard of sex behavior, and in connection with the temperance movement what would now be called "eugenic" propaganda, though the word had not then come into use. My mother saw to it that I read the pamphlets and heard the lectures pertaining to all these matters, without in the least realizing that she was thus preparing me for a radical career. I personally "sat under" Susan B. Anthony, Frances Willard, and Anna Shaw.

With this background it was inevitable that I should become a fighting feminist. But I cannot make clear my approach and method in regard to this problem of my generation without describing my own position in the family as an unwanted, a personally resented child. Probably few families in that age of enforced maternity were without some such member; but in fewer still did the intrusion take on such proportions of offense. Not that I ever blamed my mother, when I came to know them, for not wanting a child under the circumstances to which I was born. Nor do I, sorely as it hurt at the time, any longer resent that I should so early and so sharply have had my status as alien and intruder forced upon me. As you will see, it was my poor mother who lost the most in the conflict of irreconcilable temperaments never modulated by personal sympathy. Could she possibly have anticipated that I should end by being included in a list of prominent feminists, nothing would have pleased her so much; the trouble was that with that terrible pre-natal bias between us, she could never by any whipping-up of a sense of duty grow to like me, and the rest of the family took its tone from her. Long before I came to an intellectual understanding of the situation I had accepted as fact that I was not liked and could not expect the normal concessions of affection. By that adaptive instinct which still intolerably wrings my heart when I see it operating in young children, I had learned that it was only by pushing aside all considerations of liking and insisting on whatever fundamental rightness inhered in a particular situation, that I could secure a kind of factual substitute for family feeling and fair play. This began so early that though I can recall many occasions of mystified hurt at being rebuffed in the instinctive child's appeal, I can recall no time in which I did not have to conceal that hurt in order to bring all a child's wit and intelligence to bear on making good my right to be treated, factually at least, as a lawful member of the family. Out of this I developed very early an uncanny penetration into the fundamental ethics of personal situations which my mother was too just to refuse and not always clever enough to evade. By the time I was old enough to discuss our relationships with my mother the disposition to seek for logical rather than emotional elements had become so fixed that I had even made myself believe that being liked was not important. I had, at least, learned to do without it.

All this must be told in order that the bias and the method of my feminism may be understood. For life played an ironic trick on my mother. The pretty and darling daughters were taken away, and only the unwished-for ugly duckling left, between the oldest and the youngest sons. As if this were not enough, by the time the elder son was ripe for college there began to be signs that the daughter and not the son was the clever one. After my father's death mother's affectional interests, as is often the case with widows, gathered and intensified around my older brother, who proved a good son and a good citizen, but without any distinguishing gifts. When in college he had, chiefly I suspect in response to my mother's passionate wish, displayed literary and forensic tastes which he was unable to support without liberal contributions from mother and sister. These he accepted at first gingerly, and finally with such freedom that many a theme, many a quip and paragraph which appeared in the college journal over his name had been wrung out of me by such concessions as sisters do to this day obtain from older brothers by ministering to masculine complacency. Although my mother was often a party to our traffic and occasional squabbles over it, she was always able, when the things appeared, to accept them as evidence of what she so much wished. After her death I found a scrapbook in which they were all carefully arranged with my brother's name in her handwriting underneath. And lest any of the generation for whom the woman's right to the product of her own talent is completely established should think this is an unusual situation, I recommend the reading of the current if out-moded novels of that period, such, for example, as the novels of Madame Sarah Grand or May Sinclair's "Mary Olivier." For the greater part of the nineteenth century, in fact, it was not only usual but proper for parents openly to deplore that the sons had not inherited talents inconveniently bestowed upon the daughters.

I seem always to have known that I would write. Probably there was evidence of my having the necessary endowment, had there been anybody able to recognize literary talent, or tell me what to do about it. The attitude of the family was crushing. "What makes you think *you* can write?" In truth, I did not know. Looking back on the idea of a literary career which prevailed in the Middle West of that period, it was probably as well for me that nobody knew. I won a college degree by dint of insisting on it, and by crowding its four years into two and a half. My brother had the full four years. That I got so much was partly a concession to the necessity of my earning a living. With a college education I could teach, and teaching was regarded then as a liberal profession, eminently suited to women. Being plain and a little "queer," it was hoped rather than expected that I would marry. My queerness consisted, at that time, in entertaining some of the ideas that have got me elected to this list, in stoutly maintaining against all contrary opinion that I would some day write, and in the—to my family —wholly inexplicable habit of resting my case on its inherent rightness rather than upon the emotional reactions it gave rise to.

The summer I was out of college my mother decided to go West with my brother, so that he might "take up land" and grow with the country, taking me with her as being still too young for self-support. No use inquiring now whether this was a good move for me. Before the Pacific Coast filled up with Middle Westerners it was a gorgeous, an exciting place to be. Probably it proved a retardation of my literary career and a stimulus to radicalism. The immediate result was that I married. My mother had sunk all her capital in giving my brother his start; there was no place in the home for me, and no money to prepare me for any happy way of supporting myself. I taught a couple of years, not very successfully. And, anyway, I wished to be married. Contrary to the popular conception about literary women, I like domestic life and have a genuine flair for cooking. And I wanted children profoundly.

I still intended to write, but never in my life having met a professional literary person there was no one to tell me that the two things were incompatible. Under ordinary circumstances they are not. What I did not in the least realize was that the circumstances were not ordinary. I married a man with social and educational background not unlike my own; a man I could thoroughly respect for his personal quality, quite apart from any achievement. There seemed no reason why, had I been what I appeared to my family, and to my husband no doubt, the marriage should not have proved successful in every particular. What I appeared was an average young person, clever and a little odd, but not so odd that a house to keep and a baby every two years wouldn't restore me to entire normality. True, my health was not good. All my mother's babies had been sickly; I as the sickliest had always been the first to "catch" every childish ailment, and as it was not the custom in those days to send for the doctor until you knew what was the matter with the patient I seldom received medical attention. But no one had ever suggested that this need interfere with marriage and having children. It was a superstition left over from my mother's generation that ill health in women was cured by having children. Nor did I realize how compelling the creative urge would become in me. Had I even suspected it I would not have supposed it a bar to marriage. I thought that two intelligent young people could do about as they liked with life. But, like myself, my young husband was without preparation for maintaining a household. At the end of twelve years we were still living in a town of about 300 inhabitants on an income inadequate to reasonable comfort, with an invalid child.

My first baby came in the second year and left me a tortured wreck. I know now that I did not have proper medical treatment, but at the time nothing much was thought of such things. My memory of the first seven or eight years of marriage is like some poor martyr's memory of the wheel and the rack, all the best things of marriage obscured by a fog of drudgery impossible to be met and by recurrent physical anguish. For before I had discovered the worst that had happened to me I had tried a second time to have a child, unsuccessfully. Brought up as I was, in possession of what passed for eugenic knowledge, it had never occurred to me that the man I married would be less frank about his own inheritance than I had been about mine—much to his embarrassment, for nice girls were seldom frank at that time. I who had entered motherhood with the highest hopes and intentions had to learn too late that I had borne a child with tainted blood. I had to find it all out by myself. My husband's family exchanged glances, and remained silent. My mother said: "I don't know what you have done, daughter, to have such a judgment upon you." But I, brutally and indelicately, as I was given to understand, insisted upon uncovering family history until I found out. I said to my husband: "Why did you never tell me?" He said: "Because it never occurred to me." At home, he told me, they were all brought up never to refer to the obvious handicap. That was the well-bred Christian way of the 1890's. As for my own family, from beginning to end they never ceased to treat me as under a deserved chastisement.

In a way this tragic end of my most feminine adventure brought the fulfilment of my creative desire, which had begun to be an added torment by repression. Caring for a hopelessly invalid child is an expensive business. I had to write to make money. In the end I was compelled to put my child in a private institution where she was happier and better cared for than I could otherwise manage. My husband's family were good sports. They never forgot the birthdays and Christmases, and the probability that there might be normal human reactions. To my own family who demanded somewhat accusingly what they should say I said: "You can say I have lost her." Which was true and a great relief to them. My mother died shortly after, but was never quite reconciled to my refusal to accept my trouble as a clear sign of God's displeasure. So for sixteen years.

Released thus to the larger life which opened to me with literary success, I found plenty of reasons for being a feminist in the injustices and impositions endured by women under the general idea of their intellectual inferiority to men. What I have just related are the facts that gave color and direction to my feminist activities. But I must go back a little to explain the kind of thing that got me called a radical, which was not what is called a radical today. I was neither a Bolshevik nor a Communist, not even a Socialist or free lover. I thought much that was said at that time about Home and Mother, sentimental tosh; I thought it penalized married love too much to constitute the man she loved the woman's whole horizon, intellectual, moral, and economic. I thought women should be free to make their contribution to society by any talent with which they found themselves endowed, and be paid for it at rates equal to the pay of men. I thought everything worth experiencing was worth talking about; I inquired freely into all sorts of subjects. I got myself read out of the Methodist church by organizing, along in the nineties, the first self-conscious enterprise of what has been called the Little Theater movement and acting in its plays. Worst of all, I talked freely of art as though it had a vital connection with living. One example of the sort of reactions an unbridled radical such as I was had to face must suffice. That was the beginning of various movements for applying the social wisdom of the more fortunate classes to the problems of the underprivileged—juvenile courts, probation officers, big brother and sister associations, and in particular, the activity finally objectified as the court of domestic relations, in which I was particularly interested. I had spoken freely and publicly about the necessity of bringing those unlearned in life into more or less compulsory compliance with our best experience. Just why this should figure as an offense to anybody I am still at a loss to know; but the next time I went to my mother's house, I discovered that there had been a family council, and it was put to me that, while the family did not attempt to dictate what I should say away from the neighborhood of the family, I must understand that in the neighborhood, and especially under the family roof I must refrain from all mention of so objectionable a subject as public remedies for private relations, or find my mother's door forever closed to me. Not a word, you see, about the incredible private tragedy which had come to me for lack of a public remedy!.... Oh, yes, I took it, standing, for the same reason that I took it the day my pretty young sister was buried and my mother flung away from me and cried aloud on God for taking Jenny and leaving me. It wasn't until I caught the family—what was left of it— trying to put over on the younger generation the same repressions and limitations they had practiced upon me that I blew up. Suddenly I found the younger generation on my side.

As for not being under the necessity of being liked, which began as a defense, it has become part of my life philosophy. I see now that too many of the impositions of society upon women have come of their fear of not being liked. Under disguising names of womanliness, of tact, of religion even, this humiliating necessity, this compulsive fear goes through all our social use like mould, corrupting the bread of life. It is this weakness of women displayed toward their sons which has fostered the demanding attitude of men toward them. It puts women as a class forever at the mercy of an infantile expectation grown into an adult convention. So I have made a practice of standing out against male assumption of every sort, especially their assumption of the importance of masculine disapproval—more than anything else against their assumption that they have a right to be "managed." But it is the women I am aiming at, women and their need for detachment from the personal issue. At present the price for refusing to "manage" men is high, but not too high for a self-respecting woman to pay.

CRYSTAL EASTMAN

Crystal Eastman (1881-1928) was a dedicated feminist, pacifist, and socialist. After her death, Freda Kirchwey wrote, "She was for thousands a symbol of what the free woman might be." (*The Nation*, August 4, 1928) Eastman's unusual family, and especially her mother, is cited as the source of her strength and ambition. Both of her parents were Congregational ministers, who worked as the joint pastors of Park Church in Elmira, New York. Her mother, Annis Ford Eastman, was well known locally as a preacher and as an advocate of women's rights. Her younger brother, Max Eastman, became famous as a writer, crusading socialist, and editor of the radical magazine *The Liberator: A Journal of Revolution and Progress*.

Eastman was educated at Vassar College; at Columbia University, where she received a master's degree in sociology; and at New York University Law School. Living and working in New York from 1904 until the early 1920s, she became an expert on industrial accidents. She collaborated with Paul Kellogg on an important study of work accidents and the law and helped secure the passage of workmen's compensation legislation in New York state. Eastman was also a leader of the women's movement, and helped organize a number of feminist groups, including: The Congressional Union for Women's Suffrage, which became the militant Women's Party; the Women's Peace Party of New York; and the Feminist Congress of 1919. In a speech to the Feminist Congress, Eastman drew attention to many problems facing women beyond the question of the vote: unequal pay scales, discrimination against women in the labor unions, discriminatory marriage laws, economic dependence of housewives, and the unavailability of birth control information. Anticipating many of the demands of the contemporary Women's Liberation Movement, she advocated the elimination of sex roles in the family, changes in the divorce laws and in the treatment of prostitutes, payment and insurance for houseworkers, mothers' benefits, and marriage contracts.

Her mother's example influenced Eastman's passionate determination to have children as well as a career; she planned to have an illegitimate child in Italy if she was not married by her twenty-ninth birthday. But shortly before the deadline, she married Wallace Benedict, a Wisconsin insurance agent. This turned out to be an unsuccessful and childless marriage, which ended in 1915; Eastman refused alimony, explaining that "No self-respecting feminist would accept alimony. It would be her own confession that she could not take care of herself." Soon after the divorce, Eastman married Walter Fuller and went to live with him in England. She became active in the English women's movement and in the Birmingham Conference of Labour Women, a group of socialist suffragists and birth control advocates. Eastman and Fuller had two children. While she was not a doctrinaire Marxist, Eastman believed that women would be better off in a socialist society; she visited Hungary and wrote often in *The Liberator* about Russian Bolshevism.

Eastman encountered many obstacles and disappointments during her lifetime of activism. An ardent pacifist, she felt the futility of her cause during World War I. A visionary feminist, she saw the National Woman's Party ignore her broad program of education and reform, and concentrate on the Equal Rights Amendment. When she returned to America in 1927, a conservative postwar climate of opinion made it difficult for her to find work. Yet she appears to write with self-acceptance and serenity. How accurately the last paragraph of "Mother-Worship" reflects her sentiments, however, is unclear. Historian Blanche Cook has recently discovered that Eastman's original last paragraph was changed by *The Nation*, and in letters to friends and relatives, Eastman made remarks such as "It was much better as I wrote it, more honest and sure. Far more interesting."

Mother-Worship

The story of my background is the story of my mother. She was a Middle-Western girl, youngest, cleverest, and prettiest of six daughters—children of an Irish gunsmith and a "Pennsylvania Dutch" woman of good family and spendid character. The gunsmith was a master of his trade but a heavy drinker, always ugly and often dangerous. My mother got away from home as soon as she could. After a year in a nearby coeducational college she taught school for a while and then married. The man she chose (for she was the sort of girl who has many chances) was a penniless but handsome and idealistic Yankee divinity student whom she met during that one college year. When he had secured his first parish, they were married.

For about eight years, during which there were four different parishes and four children were born, my mother was a popular, active, and helpful minister's wife. Then my father, who had always struggled against ill-health, suffered a complete nervous breakdown. He was forced to give up his church and his chosen profession. My mother had to support the family.

She began by teaching English literature in a girls' school. Before long she was giving Sunday-evening talks at the school. Then she began to fill outside engagements and finally she became a sort of supply-preacher to nearby country churches. About the year 1890, though she had had no theological education, she was ordained as a Congregational minister and called to be the pastor of a fairly large church in a well-to-do farming community. After three or four successful years, she and my father (who by this time had lost a good bit of money trying to be a farmer and a grocer but had begun to regain his health) were called as associate pastors to a big liberal church in a city of 40,000. It was my mother's reputation as a preacher that brought them this opportunity and she proved equal to the larger field. In time my father's health improved so that he could carry his share of the work, but my mother was always the celebrated member of the family.

I have a vivid memory of my mother when I was six years old. We are standing, my brother and I, in front of a run-down farmhouse on the edge of the town which had become our home. We have just said goodby to our mother and now we are watching her trip off down the hill to the school where she goes every day to teach. She turns to smile at us—such a beaming smile, such a bright face, such a pretty young mother. When the charming, much-loved figure begins to grow small in the distance, my brother, who is younger and more temperamental than I, begins to cry. He screams as loud as he can, until he is red in the face. But he cannot make her come back. And I, knowing she will be worried if she hears him, try to drag him away. By the time I was ten my mother had become a preacher.

Life was never ordinary where my mother was. She was always trying something new. She had an eager, active mind, and tremendous energy. She was preeminently an initiator. From the time I was thirteen we spent our summers like most middle-class, small-town American families, in a cottage beside a lake. And our life there, I suppose, would have been much like the life in thousands of other such summer communities, except for the presence of my mother. For one thing, she organized a system of cooperative housekeeping with three other families on the hillside, and it lasted for years. A cook was hired jointly, but the burden of keeping house, planning meals, buying meat and groceries from the carts that came along three times a week, getting vegetables and fruit from the garden, collecting the money, keeping track of guests, and paying the bills, shifted every week. At first it was only the mothers who took their turn at housekeeping. But as the children grew older they were included in the scheme, boys as well as girls. Toward the end we had all the fun of eating in a big jolly group and only one or two weeks of housekeeping responsibility during the whole summer.

We used to have Sunday night music and singing for the whole hillside at our cottage, with the grown-ups in the big room, and the children lying outside on the porch couches or off on the grass. We had "church" Sunday mornings, too, in our big room; after all we were the minister's family. But it was a very short informal "church" followed by a long swim, and any one who wanted to could preach. We took turns preaching as well as at keeping house, and we could choose the subjects of our own sermons.

Then one summer my mother started "symposiums." Once a week the mothers and older children and any fathers who happened to be around would gather on somebody's porch, listen to a paper, and then discuss it. I read a paper on "Woman" when I was fifteen, and I believe I was as wise in feminism then as I am now, if a little more solemn.

"The trouble with women," I said, "is that they have no impersonal interests. They must have work of their own, first because no one who has to depend on another person for his living is really grown up; and, second, because the only way to be happy is to have an absorbing interest in life which is not bound up with any particular person. Children can die or grow up, husbands can leave you. No woman who allows husband and children to absorb her whole time and interest is safe against disaster."

The proudest and happiest moment of my college days was when I met my mother in New York, as I did once a year, and went with her to a big banquet in connection with some ministers' convention she had come down to attend. She always spoke at the banquet, and she was always the best speaker. She was gay, sparkling, humorous, intimate, adorable. I would sit and love her with all my heart, and I could feel all the ministers loving her and rejoicing in her.

Almost always it is painful to sit in the audience while a near relative preaches, prays, or makes a speech. Husbands, wives, brothers, sisters, and children of the performers ought to be exempt from attending such public functions. My brothers and I always suffered when father preached, although, as preachers go, he was pretty good. At any rate he was beautiful to look at and had a large following of enthusiastic admirers. But when my mother preached we hated to miss it. There was never a moment of anxiety or concern; she had that secret of perfect platform ease which takes all strain out of the audience. Her voice was music; she spoke simply, without effort, almost without gestures, standing very still. And what she said seemed to come straight from her heart to yours. Her sermons grew out of her own moral and spiritual struggles. For she had a stormy, troubled soul, capable of black cruelty and then again the deepest generosities. She was humble, honest, striving, always beginning again to try to be good.

With all her other interests she was thoroughly domestic. We children loved her cooking as much as we loved her preaching. And she was all kinds of devoted mother, the kind that tucks you in at night and reads you a story, and the kind that drags you to the dentist to have your teeth straightened. But I must leave her now and try to fill out the picture. My father, too, played a large part in my life. He was a generous man, the kind of man that was a suffragist from the day he first heard of a woman who wanted to vote. One evening, after mother had been teaching for some time and had begun to know her power as a public speaker, she came to him as he lay on his invalid's couch.

"John," she cried, "I believe I could preach!"

"Mary!" he cried, jumping up in his excitement, "I *know* you could!"

This was in those early days when he had given up his own career as a minister, when he had cheerfully turned small farmer and had begun, on days when he was well enough, to peddle eggs and butter at the back doors of his former parishioners. From the moment he knew that my mother wanted to preach, he helped and encouraged her. Without his coaching and without his local prestige, it is doubtful if she could have been ordained. And my father stood by me in the same way, from the time when I wanted to cut off my hair and go barefoot to the time when I began to study law. When I insisted that the boys must make their beds if I had to make mine, he stood by me. When I said that if there was dishwashing to be done they should take their turn, he stood by me. And when I declared that there was no such thing in our family as boys' work and girls' work, and that I must be allowed to do my share of wood-chopping and outdoor chores, he took me seriously and let me try.

Once when I was twelve and very tall, a deputation of ladies from her church called on my mother and gently suggested that my skirts ought to be longer. My mother, who was not without consciousness of the neighbors' opinion, thought she must do something. But my father said, "No, let her wear them short. She likes to run, and she can't run so well in long skirts."

A few years later it was a question of bathing suits. In our summer community I was a ringleader in the rebellion against skirts and stockings for swimming. On one hot Sunday morning the other fathers waited on my father and asked him to use his influence with me. I don't know what he said to them but he never said a word to me. He was, I know, startled and embarrassed to see his only daughter in a man's bathing suit with bare brown legs for all the world to see. I think it shocked him to his dying day. But he himself had been a swimmer; he knew he would not want to swim in a skirt and stockings. Why then should I?

Beyond the immediate circle of my family there were other influences at work. My mother, among her other charms, had a genius for friendship. There were always clever, interesting, amusing women coming in and out of our house. I never thought of women as dull folk who sat and listened while the men talked. The little city where we lived was perhaps unusual. It was the home of six or seven distinguished persons, and not all of them were men.

In this environment I grew up confidently expecting to have a profession and earn my own living, and also confidently expecting to be married and have children. It was fifty-fifty with me. I was just as passionately determined to have children as I was to have a career. And my mother was the triumphant answer to all doubts as to the success of this double role. From my earliest memory she had more than half supported the family and yet she was supremely a mother.

I have lived my life according to the plan. I have had the "career" and the children and, except for an occasional hiatus due to illness or some other circumstance over which I had no control, I have earned my own living. I have even made a certain name for myself. If I have not fulfilled the promise of my youth, either as a home-maker or as a professional woman, I have never wavered in my feminist faith. My mother has always been a beacon to me, and if today I sometimes feel a sense of failure it may be partly because I have always lived in the glow of her example. In their early struggle for survival against narrow-minded and prejudiced parents some of my contemporaries seem to have won more of the iron needed in the struggle of life than I got from my almost perfect parents.

11

ELIZABETH STUYVESANT

Elizabeth Stuyvesant, a dancer, settlement worker, and birth control campaigner, was one of the most radical women in the *Nation* group. She traces many of her libertarian values to her unusual family; growing up as an atheist in a small town taught her early how to live with being different. It is interesting, however, to note that all the decisions in the family were made by her father; she never mentions her mother at all. In college in Cincinnati, Stuyvesant championed the rights of Negro and Jewish students and ardently supported the suffragists. She was arrested at a violent suffrage demonstration in Washington on July 4, 1917; she was struck by a uniformed soldier and had her blouse torn off in the melee. For her part in the picketing, she was sentenced to three days in the District Jail. In New York she continued her activities as a pacifist, a feminist, and a socialist. Freedom is Stuyvesant's creed: "The utmost measure of freedom—economic, intellectual, emotional—is the *sine qua non* of the good life." Self-supporting (she worked for the New York Public Library), Stuyvesant lived her private life according to her principles, without "clerical formalities," without children, and without "the conventional idea of exclusive mutual possession."

Staying Free

I cannot explain my life without taking into account the free atmosphere which pervaded our home under the influence of my father's genuinely libertarian nature. Our home had in it absolutely no verbotens and our family grammar contained no imperative. We five boisterous children absorbed the spirit of mutual consideration without injunctions or commands.

Father's large library was open to us all at any age. We were never ordered to bed in the middle of an engrossing book but could read all night long if we wished. Dickens, Browning, and Parkman were in his library, of course, but so were Boccaccio, Rabelais, and Gulliver unabridged. And so was Lena Rivers. When we wanted the Elsie books, we got them. If my brother brought home Nick Carter and Diamond Dick they were not thrown out of the window but went the critical round of the family. When Frank Merriwell's weeklies were discovered lying about the house, my father read them aloud to us, laughing over the super-heroism but thoroughly enjoying the thrilling accounts of those olympic baseball games won by Frank and his peerless knights. When the village Comstocks were publicly condemning and secretly devouring Sappho and Camille we all read them with frank appreciation.

We always lived where there was a fireplace and almost every night found us gathered around it, listening to Grimm and the Arabian Nights, Jules Verne, Rider Haggard, Mark Twain. Father loved to read aloud, and through the long evenings in those dull, back-country places we would hear these favorites over and over. At other times he would read to us from his idols—Tom Paine, Ingersoll, Voltaire.

Early in our lives we got accustomed to being unlike other people. To be an atheist in a small town in those days was not unlike what it was to be a pacifist in 1917.

Educational opportunities in the back-water communities where we were obliged to live were so slim that our parents were deeply absorbed in the problem of our education. Various female seminaries were tried for my sisters. By the time I, the youngest, came along, my father was disgusted with the education the others had received. He hated the airs and graces taught them, the artificialities and stupidities which seemed to him so flagrant each time they came back from one of those institutions.

He took upon himself the task of my education and carried it through the grammar grades. He had many a struggle with local school boards and truant officers but always won his point by various methods of delay until his business made it necessary to move to a new community. His work was mining engineering, and he was obliged to go to any place where the company wished a mine developed. Every few years we piled everything we possessed into a freight car and away we trekked a few hundred miles into another little American wilderness. The job of carting five children and a car-load of goods across Ohio, Kentucky, and Missouri did not interrupt my father's enthusiastic

93

direction of my studies of arithmetic and grammar or his interest in my endless adventures into history and geography.

But this delightful, home-made education had its drawbacks. As I approached high-school age I began to realize this. A Christmas visit to an aunt living in a large Middle Western city, with high schools and a university, gave me the idea of going to a real school as soon as possible and then to college. This idea grew into a fixed determination. Although my desire met with no encouragement at home, I never thought of giving it up. I borrowed the railroad fare from my brother, dressed one of our fattest turkeys, packed it into an old-fashioned telescope with a bottle of home-made elder-flower wine and a jar of sausage cakes, and took a train for the city, six hundred miles away. Although my father was hurt by my going away he was remarkably generous about it; in later years he even enjoyed saying that he was a victim of his own educational methods.

During my senior year of high school, when the time came in our upper-class literary society to select from the junior class the members for the following year, I was thunderstruck to find that a colored girl, one of the most brilliant students of the school, was not even being considered. When I proposed her name the entire group disapproved violently. My chum and I made so much commotion among both students and teachers, with the staunch backing of our courageous principal, that the girl was finally admitted and proved to be one of the most popular members and an asset to the organization.

From high school I went to the university. There the sorority system struck me as being not only silly but harmful to the spirit of the institution. Jewish girls were not admitted. Poor girls needed exceptional qualities in order to run any chance of selection. On the other hand, "dumb-bells" were fought over if their fathers were wealthy or their mothers socially prominent. When rushing time came I turned down the bids I received, to the astonishment of the whole student body, even those most discriminated against.

Women at the time were not allowed to take courses in the medical school of the university—a holy place, sacred to the male students. My high-school chum and I were especially interested in biology and we wished to supplement our studies with a course in bacteriology given only in the medical school. We tried to register for this course but were diplomatically refused. We insisted upon the right to take any course offered by the university. The authorities put us off with that paternal condescension with which the requests of women used to be disposed of. We tried to get other girls in the biology course to back us. They laughed at us. We took it up with some of the men in the bacteriological class. They welcomed us and supported our demand. In the end we marched triumphantly into the bacteria laboratory, and since then courses in that medical school have been open to all students.

Suffrage, at that time, had emerged from the stage of ignorant misrepresentation but was going through a period in some ways more discouraging—supercilious toleration. Most of our classmates were bored by the subject and ignored it. My chum's mother had been a pioneer with Elizabeth Cady Stanton and Anna Shaw and had passed on the enthusiasm of that experience to her daughter. One memorable day we learned that Mrs. Pankhurst had come to America. Eagerly we telegraphed the great militant, asking if she would speak at our college. Nothing can ever match the exhilaration of arranging the meeting for our heroine, advertising it among the students, and making her stay among us count to the utmost for the cause. It was then that I had my first sense of being a part of something fine moving in the world.

On leaving the university, the natural step in those days for a self-supporting woman was into social work. There, even more than in school and college, the frank and free home atmosphere which had been my luck proved its worth. Brought face to face with the ugliest facts of life as a case worker in the red-light district of a cosmopolitan city, the callow college graduate was able to maintain a scientific attitude tempered with human sympathy. It was not long before I became the executive head of one of the many charities of the city, all federated and super-federated into one great philanthropic whole. I was the angel child of a charming group of elderly Lady Bountifuls who adored my dramatic reports of the misery among the special type of poor they had elected to help. But the mitigation of suffering, even under such delightful auspices, began to pall. Like so many others, I wanted to go deeper.

There was probably never a time when the air was so charged with social currents. Civic-reform leagues were active. Muckraking and trust-busting had not gone out of fashion. Single tax held a serious place in the discussions of thoughtful students of society. Prison reform had been given great impetus by the exposures of Thomas Mott Osborne, and the probation system was being widely adopted. Sex hygiene had graduated from the stage of a hobby, and birth control was a question to be courageous about. In this ferment of ideas my well-established habit of intellectual hospitality led me step by step to more fundamental philosophies. The entrance to this new world was through the home of a strong but gentle anarchist woman, whose two children pluckily bore her name amid the ignorant jeers of their schoolmates. My thinking was profoundly affected by those evenings at her home with a group of choice souls out of that smug, crass, over-uplifted, over-settlement-housed city—a printer who would handle only beautiful, intelligent things, using none but the finest paper and the most artistic type faces; a bookseller whose shop was the only place where one could buy the *Masses, Freedom, Bruno's Weekly;* a few foreign-born workers from the local steel mills, vibrant, earnest idealists of the type who would neither scab in a strike nor take part in a war; a dancing teacher, fresh from the influence of Isadora Duncan, making a daring struggle for beauty and self-expression. I joined her class and wrote indignant letters to the local papers defending her work when the Purity League and the Daisy Chainers would have driven her out of town.

At this stimulating stage Lochinvar arrived, not out of the West but from my own immediate milieu—the executive head of one of the leading philanthropic organizations of the city. He also was realizing the futility of social palliatives and was having difficulties with his directors because of his too frank exposure of local industrial and housing conditions and his ardent interest in the anti-preparedness agitation. About this time I was warned by my lady managers that my enthusiasms were carrying me too far. These official mutterings, however, did not deter either one of us.

Lochinvar's difficulties inevitably increased. He finally received an abrupt notice of dismissal and we decided to go to New York to live. We have never regretted giving up the secure life of the social worker for the rough and tumble struggle for existence which is the lot of most self-supporting people. My real life seemed only then to begin. It was entirely honest, it was a full life, and it was my own.

The country was then wallowing in the war orgy. There were raids, arrests, imprisonment. Radical leaders were being tried for publishing a magazine, writing a book, or making a speech. Employers' associations, with the aid of complaisant district attorneys, were squaring old accounts with union organizers. Whether it was building up a defense organization, preparing a gigantic protest meeting against conscription, or attempting to elect Morris Hillquit mayor of New York, I was there.

It was the most logical thing in the world that I should join in the militant suffrage activity at Washington, do my time in jail, and win my badge of honor. What a glorious company of emancipated women they were! There was not one of us who did not come out of that experience with less awe of policeman, judge, and established ideas and with a clearer understanding of the true nature of authority.

I did not tarry long in the doctrinaire stage of those who "belong" to this or that. After the tumult and the shouting of 1916-1920 died down, it was possible to think out the fundamentals. I understood better what the printer and the bookseller and those steel-workers were aiming at. The utmost measure of freedom—economic, intellectual, emotional—is the *sine qua non* of the good life.

In the more intimate application of this philosophy, eleven years of a free and uninterruptedly happy association surely prove something. We have never felt the need to sanctify our union with lay or clerical formalities. There is a rare spiritual value in the consciousness that mutual desire is the only tie that binds. Nor have we been willing to cut down our freedom in order to increase the census figures. With "childless old age" not so very far away, we still maintain that there is more genuine companionship to be had with chosen friends of similar age and experience than with immature fledglings of another generation.

As I look back over our eleven happy years I feel sure that our relationship would not have been so harmonious or complete if either of us had stressed the conventional idea of exclusive mutual possession. As my own thinking grows I am finding it quite conceivable that there may be room in my life for other close relationships. Deep human affection is a rich source of happiness in this drab world. Women are finding out this great truth and are accepting it.

LOU ROGERS

Unlike most of the women in *The Nation* series, Lou Rogers, a political cartoonist and illustrator, describes her childhood as joyous and exuberant. Her family encouraged self-reliance and freedom of choice for both sons and daughters; their unconditional love and support seem to have given Rogers a special kind of self-confidence. With a woman friend she organized a physical-culture tour of the Far West, an adventure that ended in hilarious disaster. She survived rejection by New York editors and art school teachers, and although she talks of being desperate, ragged, and hungry, her zest and resilience dominate her narrative. In the 1920s, Rogers was a member of Heterodoxy. She was best known for her "Gimmicks"—illustrated verses about mischievous gnomes which appeared regularly in the *Ladies Home Journal*. She also illustrated children's books about her beloved North Woods.

Two of the psychologists singled Rogers out for comment in their analyses of the series. Joseph Collins found her the most attractive of all the Modern Women, the one who, in his fantasies, he would most like to know. "She seems to have neither ambition nor determination to administer the world, and she knows how to laugh and be joyous," he wrote. Beatrice Hinkle recognized something quiet different in Rogers: a woman who had fulfilled herself unselfconsciously. She compared Rogers to Elizabeth Stuyvesant, seeing them both as women whose feminism "was not born out of a sense of injustice and bitterness, but developed as a natural growth from their own personality in contact with the special family environment." Very much an individualist, Rogers felt happy with her life in 1927 and in her conclusion suggests that "the spirit of cooperation," rather than social or economic changes, could help other women make successes of their lives.

Lightning Speed Through Life

We always have been and are now a family of laughers. When father and mother and the seven children with the grandchildren gather each fall in the family camp on the lake shore in northern Maine, we do more laughing in two hours than lots of families do in six months.

There are several reasons for the laughter that has always welled up through our family relations like a clear spring. Perhaps the main reason is that father and mother have loved each other with a feeling that runs through the whole structure of their emotional and mental beings, not a consuming passion but a living and powerful reality. I have never heard them quarrel. Sometimes one turned upon the other with a burst of passionate impatience, but even now when they are far along in years—father is eighty-seven—these occasional gusts end in a quaint bit of humor like a rainbow.

My forebears on both sides were pioneers of New England stock. My paternal grandfather was a doctor, and one of the founders of the village in northern Maine which was, until recent years, a lumber-supply center for the lumbering operations to the north and west. He and a handful of other college-educated men founded the academy, the library, and the churches, and ran the affairs of the town in the days when northern Maine depended for its communications on stage routes through unbroken forest. He was a little man who drove through the woods at a great pace in a very high, two-wheeled untopped gig, hitched to a dappled mare named Nell. Under the seat was a bag of little black pills.

Father was until recently more than six feet tall with a splendid physique, dark eyes and hair, a commanding personality, and what is called in the town "the family gift for gab." He was not a student and did not go to college, but he has been a thinker after his original fashion all his life. He reaches his conclusions as the crow flies, and they are sound and logical.

Mother's people were ship-builders and farmers. Her father, a West Point graduate, was killed when she was very small. She lived with her grandfather, who used to clear a fine farm, plant it to small fruits, and then get rid of it to start all over again on another spot. There are in mother fine feeling, innate reasonableness, gentle under-standing of people, and a love of beautiful and gracious things. She has a swift, buoyant spirit, intrepid but with some shyness in it, as if her solitary childhood in the depths of forest country had left its touch upon her. Her schooling was not much, but she has read and studied and gathered knowledge from every direction until she is one of the most well-informed persons I know. Physically she has always had great recuperative power. If this had been lacking she would have succumbed to the amount of manual labor that always confronted her.

As a family, we lived all the life there was to be lived in the community, on the farm, and in the woods. Money was scarce—the only rugs we ever had were moose and deer skins and a chance nickel looked as big as a straw bed—but I do not see how with money we could have got more out of our surroundings. Father was for many years a lumberman in the woods around Katahdin and to the north of it. We children, four boys and three girls, spent our vacations in the string of lumber camps. It never seemed to occur to anybody that girls didn't do everything that boys did. Nobody ever followed us around or suggested fear to us. We were expected to use good judgment and keep our wits sharp. Guns, canoes, axes were utensils to use and handle with skill whenever we had need of them. We met the test of endurance at every hand.

In all that woods life—from the winter camps with their vigorous activities to the spring drives of logs with crashing white waters, log-jams, the ringing bing of cant dogs, dams with their roaring sluice-ways—we children belonged, not so much looking on as feeling part and parcel of it. And back on the farm, with woods on four sides of it, we belonged too. We worked hard and played hard, and all the children in the neighborhood were welcome to come and play with us.

We were always going off on camping expeditions of various kinds —and are yet, for that matter. Piling on buckboards behind teams of horses with tent and food; spending a week or two on some distant lake shore, or back over the tote roads to the fire-swept Wissattaquoik Valley for blueberries; on to a Grand Army encampment, for father was a Civil War veteran, or to a country fair perhaps. All expeditions that filled us youngsters with joy as well as the several neighbors' children who went along. And Thanksgiving and Christmas were gorgeous feasts; the relatives all gathered to make holiday, and being a hearty folk, they loved fun as well as a groaning board.

My parents both had the old New England ideal of responsibility for public affairs and were leaders in church and town activities, working tooth and nail for the things they believed in. We children shared in discussions of these questions, as well as of national politics. We had current magazines and papers and a good supply of books. We had to attend church and Sunday school as long as we lived at home, but we were never urged to join the church. My parents's religious belief is a real thing to them, but it has no bigotry. They never tried to force it down our throats, nor did they any other belief. As I feel back along my childhood I am not conscious of any galling strain, but rather a rapid movement of prodigious and wholesome vigor. Father and mother succeeded in leaving us children a wide freedom of choice. After I left home it never occurred to me to lay any of my decisions before my parents nor did it ever occur to me that their disagreements with my decisions or ways of life could make any real difference in their feeling toward me.

With a few dollars earned by teaching a back-district school—I added some by building my own fires and chucking the wood in through the schoolhouse window—I started forth into the world to seek my fortune. As a small child I decided, one day, to learn to dive. I went out by myself in a canoe to a raft we had in the middle of a bottomless cove, clambered up the springboard, and dived straight down into the black water. If my fears had got the best of me I should have drowned, but they didn't. In much the same way I plunged into the world.

My first venture was ringing the bell of the great door in the Massachusetts Normal Art School in Boston. Our schools at home had no drawing at all, but by making caricatures of the teachers on the blackboards—and being put in the corner therefor—I had discovered a little talent. I had an idea that by training this a bit I might help myself through college. This particular door of the Normal Art School was most imposing and was used only on state occasions; but I didn't know that and rang away at the bell. A six-foot Negro—the first I'd ever seen —opened the door, finally, and stared down at me with bulging eyes. "Was dat you makin' all dat ringin'!" he exclaimed, taking in my diminutive figure in impossible country clothes, "I t'ought 'twas a fire!"

I stayed in that school as long as my money lasted, which was not long. I did not get much out of it. The life of the great city interested me so passionately that I had little time to spend in the musty depths of the school. I hated the plinths and the dead white casts and the stiff designs for wall-paper. One instructor's phrase did become a part of my equipment and has stuck to me like a good angel ever since: I had chased a circus parade through Chinatown when I should have been preparing for an examination; consequently I failed. When I told my charcoal teacher about it he said heartily, "Don't let a little thing like that bother you."

I finally gave up my college ambitions for two reasons: I failed the preliminary examinations—mischief had played a bigger part in my school days than application—and I became obsessed with the idea of teaching an elocution and physical culture system that an Armenian preacher in our town had introduced to me. Having earned half the money necessary to get to Washington, D.C., where the school was located, I borrowed the rest from a Canadian woodsman and departed. My scientist brother, living in Washington, investigated the school and reported it mostly fake, but I entered just the same.

The head of this establishment, learning of my brother's condemnation, took out his wrath on me. He was rascal enough to refuse me admittance to the two classes for which I had paid tuition until I had paid cash tuition for all the classes there were. Somehow I raised the money. It was a disagreeable year, but at the end came an episode that eased my sore heart. Twice in the season the school gave a public performance. The head attempted to shut me out of these, but one of the teachers, a most noble and gifted woman, put me into the final exhibition in spite of him. I wrote my own recitation, a piece that called for character work and humor. It made a huge hit and brought encore after encore. After that requests to recite came from organizations all over the city; so that I left the school with its owner flat as a pancake and my own soul filled with satisfaction.

With a girl I had met in the school I decided, at the close of the season, to go West from Chicago and organize physical-culture classes from town to town. We reached Chicago and our last penny at the same moment. My friend was pretty and amiable but quite unwilling to stand the gaff of hard work, so I undertook to support both of us. We were young, and this expedition covering the better part of a year was a great adventure. We pawned and sold our clothes, and I dipped candy in a chocolate factory, became an expert waitress, clerked in a hotel, and succeeded in organizing physical-culture classes which were big enough to support one but not two.

We put through one enterprising job in a Far Western city that I still think was not so bad for two inexperienced backwoodsmen. It would have turned out well, too, if I had known more about business. We took a whole suite in a leading hotel, went to the best stationer, and had handsome cards printed; we hired the swellest carriages possible and, having found out who were the leaders of society, made calls upon them. Incredible as it sounds, since we had no money and the shabbiest clothes you ever saw, we induced the ladies we called on to be patronesses of a public demonstration of physical culture set to music. We hired a hall and invited the general public, announcing the performance by lively posters.

The hall was crowded. As a result I got a fine class and aroused considerable excitement even among the Mormon elders. Unfortunately I failed to charge enough for the lessons to meet the bills. I just managed to finish the course. By that time the hotel threatened arrest and seized our luggage. We cared little about that because there was nothing inside it. I tried to meet the calamity, but failed; and one night we both quietly slipped out of town. Long afterward I paid my share of those bills.

Soon after this tramp adventure I decided to be a cartoonist—a real political cartoonist. I came to New York without a cent and without knowing a soul. I was unskilled. I had not the slightest idea how to tap the city's resources. I was certain of only one thing: I would be a cartoonist. I did almost everything from working in a disreputable prize-package factory on the East Side to selling Woodrow Wilson's "History of the American People" in instalments on West End Avenue. I was often ragged and cold and heartsick and hungry, but after a while I began to get the lay of the land. I attempted to invade the sacred precincts of the big newspapers. I tried Arthur Brisbane over and over, until the youngsters in the outer office grinned at me in derision. One day I sat down and wrote a letter to Mr. Brisbane. I told him I had come to the city to earn money as a cartoonist in order that I might raise the mortgage from the old farm in Maine; that I had no training or money but that I did have some cartoons that I should like to lay before him. The mortgage story was a whopper, but it fetched Mr. Brisbane by the next mail. With what an air I presented myself and my invitation to the dragons at the entrance need not be described. Mr. Brisbane was gentle and kind. He looked at my stuff and suggested that I could undoubtedly raise the mortgage much more quickly by going back to Maine. He said that newspapers had no use for women in this particular line of work and not much use for them in any other.

Life got pretty desperate. I had heard of a teacher at the Art Students League whose criticisms were so harsh that he was not allowed to teach women's classes. I am sure now that this was not so, but I thought: "Now, that's the very man I'll go to. He'll tell me the truth." So I took my sketches under my arm and went to the League. I waited in the half-light on the stair-landing for this man on whom I had pinned my faith. Finally he came up the stairs, a slight man with head bent. Timidly I accosted him: If some time he was at leisure would he give me some advice? I was not a student there. "Of course!" he said as if he'd been waiting for me to ask him, "why not, right now, this minute?" He took me into the members' room, and looked at my sketches. What he said warmed my heart as nothing ever had before or has since.

"You have the talent of one in twenty thousand!" he said. He told me he was giving me the benefit of many years of newspaper experience when he added, "Newspapers have no use for women in this field; your row will be a hard one. Keep out of art schools, pick up what knowledge you need, and keep at it." I was still in a way as much at sea as ever, only now I had a reason for sticking.

In the place where I lived was a college-bred woman who bitterly hated the suffrage cause. Until I listened to her railings I really never knew there was such a thing. Now it did make an impression. I hunted up a street-corner speaker, got some literature and read it, and on the instant knew I belonged. There was no bitterness in my soul, just a recognition of the need to help men and women change their focus a bit. I still knew little about drawing, but I saw that there was not a cartoon on our side, though plenty of fierce ones on the other. I made a sketch in ink of a man standing in a most conceited attitude with both feet on the ballot box holding against his breast a diploma marked "Past master in egotism"; I drew huge donkey's ears on his head and under it I put the caption: "The ballot box is mine, because it's mine."

I went with this to suffrage headquarters. Dr. Anna Howard Shaw's experience with cartoons had been very unhappy. I am sure this unladylike picture filled her with horror. It was certainly not welcome, and I took it to the New York *Call*. The editor literally hugged me! Next day the thing came out on the front page—and a full page at that! I still have the proof, and after all this time I find it not so bad.

Whether in the years since then I have accomplished anything worth while or not, I have thoroughly enjoyed living. Love is no stranger to me. My love affairs began in childhood and have been going on ever since in varying kinds and with as many results. Love is good wherever it comes from. I am married now, and I find that good, too. Economic freedom is good, and I still have it. But it seems to me that in these days of rapidly increasing fair play between a man and a woman neither economic dependence or independence makes much difference. It is the spirit of cooperation that counts and enables two people to make adjustments both inside and outside of their relationship.

I don't know exactly what people mean by disillusionment. I love to live and the longer I keep at it the greater capacity I have for living, and when I die, if it be so arranged that I lose my individual entity, I pray that I may become the lightning that snaps and crackles and whips through a thunder-storm.

PHYLLIS BLANCHARD

Phyllis Blanchard (1895-), a distinguished child psychologist, used her essay to describe her "long struggle between my own two greatest needs—the need for love and the need for independence." Like Lorine Pruette, Blanchard's early views on men and marriage were determined by the negative experience of her parents' unhappy marriage and eventual divorce. She vowed never to marry and never to "give any man an opportunity to ruin my life." Sex, she thought, "was a degrading and disgusting phenomenon which men enjoyed but to which women submitted only because it was a part of wifely duty." But upon graduating from New Hampshire State University in 1917, she, like Pruette, went to Clark University, receiving her Ph.D. in psychology in only two years. At Clark she worked with G. Stanley Hall; read Freud, Adler, Jung, Havelock Ellis, and Ellen Key; and accepted, after much conflict, that "a normal sex life for women was a scientific fact." At Clark she also met Walter Lucasse, a graduate student in chemistry. They were married in 1925 and settled in Philadelphia, where he taught at the University of Pennsylvania and she began a long and successful career with the Child Guidance Clinic.

Blanchard's feminist philosophy has much in common with Lorine Pruette's, but she is more optimistic about women's ability to integrate the two demands of life into a healthy psyche. In *The Adolescent Girl* (1920) she writes:

True feminism. . . . is based on the assumption that woman has a right to demand that she be assured adequate expression of her love and sympathy, whether in the family circle or in the mothering of world affairs for the welfare of society and the race. . . . Only as she gives herself over unreserved to these deeper motives of her physiological and psychological makeup. . . only as she obeys the intuitive guidance of the unconscious, can she find herself truly in harmony with the fundamental laws of the great cosmic process.

The Long Journey

Farm life in New England is—or was, before the day of the automobile —lonely and isolated enough at best. Picture its overwhelming loneliness for a child without brothers and sisters, who had to trudge a mile and a half to the one-room country school where some fifteen or twenty pupils gathered to learn the three R's—and little else. Only twenty years ago the round of my existence was from such a home to such a school; yet for the last ten years I have been a city dweller, readily adapting myself to conditions in crowded centers of population. Has this experience been simply a part of the general urban drift of rural youth? Perhaps, but as I look back it seems to me that I can discern certain specific influences which were operating even in those early days to shape my maturity.

The lack of playmates forced me to find many of my childhood satisfactions in a land of make-believe. I kept imaginary playmates to a much later age than do most children, and began day-dreaming long before the period of adolescence. Perhaps this over-development of my imaginative life made it easy for me to share my mother's world of dreams with her. My mother was not happy in her own life; she would have escaped from the dull routine and hard labor of the farm had she been able. Her one consolation was the determination that her daughter should have the things for which she had longed so passionately. In our talks together she dwelt upon her desire that I should not be tied down to household cares and that I should follow a professional career, as many of my other relatives had done. Through her descriptions I became well acquainted with Great-aunt Abbie, who was a pioneer schoolmistress; with Cousin John, who was a professor in a famous university, and with Cousin Josiah, who was a specialist in children's diseases in Boston. I sometimes think these never-seen individuals became more real to me than the neighbors and farmhands whom I saw daily.

At any rate, my day-dreams and ambitions fell docilely into line with my mother's aspirations for me. I never pictured the romantic episodes or the domestic scenes which are the subjects of most maiden reveries. I was not sure what I should do when I grew up, but I was determined to gain a position worthy of the many important figures in my mother's family. I, too, would win fame by virtue of high achievement. I have a tender feeling for those young illusions. I have none left in these days of facing reality, but without the driving power of such dreams I might have accomplished even less.

My parents were unhappily married. From this reality I was not guarded. Popular books in the field of child study were not available at that time, and my mother, in unburdening her mind to me, probably had no conception of the effect her confidences had. In all the struggles between my father and my mother I identified myself completely with her, and always thought him in the wrong. One day I heard her tell him that only the thought of my welfare prevented her from seeking a divorce. I solemnly assured her that I, too, could do without him, and from then on I continually urged her to follow this course. When I was a sophomore in high school my mother acted upon this advice, and the figure of my father passed out of our lives.

But the shadow of those early experiences darkened my attitude toward men and marriage long after. I was sure that I should never marry, never give any man an opportunity to ruin my life. My mother upheld me in these views. By the time I lost this support through going away to college I had read enough feminist literature and studies on marriage to encourage an opinion which had its origin in my early emotional experiences.

My mother was, without doubt, the source of a driving ambition which was sufficiently strong to buoy me up through periods of ill-health or of economic stress. But the antagonism toward men which she had also fostered dwarfed and warped my emotional development. Insistence upon one goal—the attainment of distinction by my own efforts without the need to love, honor, or obey any man—became the guiding fiction to which I tried to shape my life. The result was continual rebellion against things as they were.

As long as I believed, in harmony with my early teaching, that sex was a degrading and disgusting phenomenon which men enjoyed but to which women submitted only because it was a part of wifely duty, the appeal of celibacy and independence was enhanced. But with the biology and psychology courses of college and university, sex took on a new meaning. It was probably as much of a shock to me to learn that women had their share of the sexual instincts and emotions as it was to many of my classmates to come into contact with philosophical doubts concerning the religious views which they had unquestioningly accepted. My own churchgoing had been at a minimum, indulged in purely at my own whim and inclination, so that I was able to slough off what little superstition I had acquired without any sense of discomfort. But to readjust my ideas and my philosophy to a world which had suddenly lost its feminine integrity, and in which women needed men even as men needed women, was a serious matter.

It took many hours and days of reading to furnish me with a background against which I could evolve a new philosophy to settle this conflict. Westermarck, Crawley, Freud, Adler, Jung, Havelock Ellis, and Ellen Key became my daily familiars. At last I emerged with a modified viewpoint. The necessity of a normal sex life for women was a scientific fact, and I must bow to the truths established by science. I was not, however, compelled to accept the institution of marriage, which was plainly a lineal descendant of primitive rites and ceremonials having its beginnings in ideas of magic later carried over into the folkways and mores. I could recognize that I had normal sex emotions but I need not give up my freedom and independence by submitting to any such religious or legal ceremony. By this formula, I was able to preserve my guiding fiction intact.

It is amusing, now, to look back on this process of reassurance. Men and women are inevitably possessed of a power over each other which cannot be thought out of existence or evaded by refusing to legalize a relationship. Whether or not it is conventionalized, love has a coercive effect upon individual behavior; refusal of marriage cannot alter this fact. My fine theories, which were only attempts to effect a reconciliation of my natural longing for love with my desire for personal autonomy, never stood the test of experience. Once or twice I was tempted to relinquish my profession for the ancient position of woman as wife, but the spirit of independence was too strong. I might play with the idea of submission to masculine authority, but at the first sign of any real or permanent enslavement I shrank away and clung to my liberty. There was always my work to stabilize me in these crises. And as steadily as if there had been no such thing in the world as unsatisfied emotions, I won professional advancement. The loss of dear companionship could be forgotten after a time, in the world of books waiting to be read or to be written; my feelings were eased tremendously by writing.

The long struggle between my own two greatest needs—the need for love and the need for independence—probably had its effect upon my final choice of a profession. I had originally intended to write, but the drive to understand human motives and conduct, which arose out of the necessity of solving my own problems, developed into a desire to understand all behavior, and I turned to the social sciences. Probably this was a happy decision. Had I been only a writer, I might have prolonged indefinitely my separation from reality. Through a more scientific approach, I began to see things as they actually were rather than as I wished them to be. I even came to understand that in spite of the intensity of my feeling about marriage I might be able to accept the outward form so long as the inner spirit of the relationship embodied freedom. Thus, at thirty, I went forth to meet the fate which I had so long feared—and found it good!

It is fortunate for me that this venture has been with a man of insight, imagination, and humor, who cherishes no desire to be owner or tyrant. He respects my work as much as I do his. If he does not feel quite so keenly as I the need of econcomic independence after marriage, he is more eager that I have leisure for creative work than I am myself. Nor is this because my writings bear witness that I am his wife, for I keep my own name. To us, marriage is no sacred bond which it would be a sacrilege to sever. Rather, we regard it as a form to which we have submitted because it is the only way in which we can give expression to our love without interference. With marriage, thus interpreted, I am content. It is as if I had accomplished the impossible feat of eating my cake and having it—for I have both love and freedom, which once seemed to me such incompatible bedfellows.

VICTORIA McALMON

Victoria McAlmon, a teacher and radical, was the oldest of eight children of a Presbyterian minister. Her youngest brother, Robert McAlmon, was a poet, novelist, and celebrity of the twenties, a member of the expatriate Lost Generation of Fitzgerald and Hemingway. The McAlmons grew up in the Middle West, moving from Kansas to South Dakota, and finally to Minneapolis around 1910. Despite the family's intellectual and liberal spirit, the McAlmon girls had fewer opportunities for education and self-development than their brothers. Victoria had to delay college, although her father and all her brothers were university educated. She attended and taught at the State Normal School in Madison, South Dakota, and then borrowed money to go to the University of Chicago. Later she did graduate work in vocational guidance at the University of Minnesota.

McAlmon's liberalism found expression in a variety of professional and political activities. For many years she worked for the Minneapolis school system, as a teacher of history and English, and as social worker for the Board of Education. She was a Charter Member of the Minneapolis Federation of Teachers; the first president of the Minneapolis Women's Trade Union League; vice-president of the Minnesota Non-Partisan

Working People's League; and, as a delegate from the teachers' union, vice-president of the Minneapolis Trades and Labor Assembly. Her work with organized labor, she writes in her essay, "has captivated and held me. Like everything else that I have gone in for it is not enough, but I can find nothing better or more fundamental in our national life to which I can be attached."

In 1923, McAlmon went to England to visit her brother and his wife, the novelist Bryher (Winifred Ellerman), and to study the British Labour party. She attended the Fabian school, and met Beatrice and Sidney Webb as well as Labour party politicians. Returning to Minneapolis in 1924, she became a candidate for Congress on the Farmer-Labor ticket, the only woman candidate in Minnesota. Organized in 1918, the Farmer-Labor party won more elections than any other third party in American history, but its coalition of socialists, workers, and small farmers was constantly under attack from business and the press. McAlmon lost the election, and in 1930 she was fired from her job because of her political activities. Joining her mother and married sister in Los Angeles, she took a job as director of guidance and placement at Los Angeles City College. After her retirement, McAlmon traveled to Europe and Mexico and remained interested in politics. She died in 1969.

Free—For What?

I was born in a British colony and transported early to the Middle Western part of the United States, where I have lived most of four decades. My witty, well-educated, clerical father moved his family frequently from one home mission field to another to the joy of his gipsyish offspring and the distress of his wife, who wished to settle and rear their large family where good schools and gracious people were. We had to restrain the baby from saying in public: "Papa, I want to move again. When are we going to move?"

The philosophy of family life as enunciated by my father ran something like this: Because we were superior people—just why I did not know—we must behave extremely well. We must get the best grades in school, we must be mannerly and well informed, we must, while on duty as clergyman's children, conceal the spirits that were endured—and sometimes enjoyed and fostered—at home. Some important things to know were: Only badly informed persons believed in a protective tariff. Parnell was magnificent and when he fell the world was set back fifty years. Woman suffrage was right and girls were as clever as boys, but they must prove it. Prohibition probably never would come but one should work for it, and the saloon was evil. Europe—Sweden especially—managed the liquor question better. People who believed in the millennium were asses. The plutocracy of the United States is far more dangerous, as time will show, than is the aristocracy of Europe. Americans are fine hospitable people who have not read history or studied logic. One must learn to argue, and if worsted must not lose one's temper or cry.

My mother bore too many children. Her daughters were fairly well treated, but she was too Christianly submissive. She did not have the joy in battle that most of her offspring had. Her children were always fiercely her partisans but grew to think her troubles were of her own making, though inescapably so.

My mother was a pretty literal Christian. She grieved when we told lies. She talked to us about turning the other cheek and sometimes for love of her we tried this experiment. Once I asked her if I could ever be beautiful like my lovely sister, and she said I could not because my eyes, my hair, my skin could never equal Jane's. I could, however, be remarkable for goodness. I tried for twenty-four hours to practice this awful goodness in which you search your wicked heart for evil thoughts. I wound up by throwing a fork at a brother and rejoicing that it stood up on his coat shoulder with the prongs in the cloth, maybe even in him. I was completely done with such goodness. In order that we might look well-dressed mother turned, dyed, remade, and ornamented clothes for years. We did not, as mother would have, tell inquisitive people, a clergyman's affairs being everybody's business, that our aunts sent us clothing, blankets, table linen. Instead, my sister and I would reply to questions with a succession of contradictory fibs and titter, "One of the answers is true. Guess which."

Because we never remained long in one place we escaped much conformity. We enjoyed the histrionic aspect of our lives. Clergymen and their families can never be as righteous as they are supposed to be. When my father peevishly went back on his principles and treated us unjustly, we told him he was a hypocrite; but when he attempted for the sixth time to give up his secret smoking his children urged him not to do this.

There was often excellent talk at home. The educated and free-thinking men and women of the community frequented our place. My father argued on all sides of every subject. Usually, we had the best library in the small towns in which we lived. The village atheist and my father had a covert fondness for each other. I still wonder why this skeptical, able man was not more ambitious. Why was he content to be a home missionary, wasting his energies on the aid society, the choir, the missionary society? It may have been an Old World delight in leisure, in freedom to read and to meditate. Maybe he was one of the thousands of seeming misfits in life, whose misplacement was heightened by a dependence upon the Lord, which is only a disguise for laziness. He had not always been lazy. He had left Ireland when twelve years old and had earned his way by teaching through Knox College in Toronto and through Princeton in the United States. He had felt "called" to home missionary work and it seemed to me had failed to do much for himself or for others in it.

Much that was joyous in life we early learned must be arrived at deviously. Every congregation had its cranks who supped at our house and aired their theories. The godly might not dance, flirt, or play cards. Did my parents know that I read George Eliot, an author who was a disreputable woman, such a guest inquired one night. Horror made my food tasteless. My father said he did not disapprove of this reading although he had not known of it. After supper he would read to the guest some pages showing her how moralistic this author was. I had to kneel and endure the indecency of hearing my brother prayed over by a caller who had come to complain that Duncan had fought when "preacher's son" was called after him in a new school. After the sudden death of this brother my father no longer asked his other sons not to defend themselves.

We children became adepts at selecting our kind in each new town into which we moved. Our kind were the lively and loyal, whose environment was like ours or who could be counted on to join us in concealing a common guilt. We fetched treasures with us which made for popularity—a strangely marked cat, a tailless hen, white mice, a lame dog, a canary, and seven and finally eight of ourselves. Sometimes while paint was drying in the parsonage we were distributed as guests in various homes. When we foregathered again my second brother had the nucleus of his gang, my pretty sister her following, and I, the oldest, had learned who were the *unco guid* and who might be fellow-sinners.

Because I must not dance the dances that I went to can never be equaled on this side of paradise. Once after choir practice the beau whom my mother most approved called to get my raincoat and to tell her that I was spending the night with Mary Cleveland, an elder's daughter. I did go, but not until 4 a.m., after a dance, and I woke jerkily at intervals to wonder what would happen should a pillar in the church tell my father on me.

I read much. I perceived hypocrisy speedily and despised all but my own practices of it. I did my duty by the Sunday school, the Christian Endeavor Society, and prayer meeting because I tacitly admitted that these were my jobs and not bad ones when embroidered with sociability. I learned not to repeat my father's remarks after observing his handsome apology occasioned by my babbling. He had made, he confessed, the remarks about Mrs. Jordan's purple hat and triple chins. It was not Christ-like and it was ungentlemanly. He asked her pardon for this and hoped she would blame him entirely and not his little daughter, who had told only the truth. He walked into his study after the episode without reproaching me and left me stricken with shame and moved to my depths with admiration. For weeks I did not say he was a hypocrite.

When I finished high school at sixteen there was no money to send me to college, so I taught a country school and met with what I then thought a burning injustice. This was supposed to be a difficult school and the directors doubted if a woman could manage it. The sons of two of these trustees jumped out of a window when kept after school for some disobedience. My discipline was wrecked if I could not dominate the situation. After the morning exercises I sent the two muscular young corn-huskers to get a switch. They brought a proper one, but the more knavish boy would not, for half an hour, let me punish him. Everyone knew that, strong young tomboy that I was, I could not thrash him unless he would consent. I conquered him by sticking to the project until he gave up and agreed that he was in the wrong. I punished him hard, and then more lightly hurt his disciple. I was sick at heart about it all day because I had played pull away and other games with these boys daily, and their folly was mere boyish bravado. However, there was no doubt in anyone's mind that this affair was intended to try me out. The farmer at whose house I boarded had told me, what I sensed myself, that I must win in the struggle or resign. The next day, a peaceful one, the three farmer directors stalked majestically into the schoolroom. After the pupils left, the father of the more stubborn boy scolded me for whipping his son. He conceded grudgingly that the boy should not disobey and that he should be punished, but he growled sullenly that I should not have done it. I was amazed to hear myself saying passionately: "You talk to me like this because I am a woman. A man would knock you down." My three guests filed mutely out. The director could not endure the laughter that followed the story as embellished by his associates and he resigned.

Later I went to one of the dismal normal schools that flourished throughout the country twenty years ago. I had read more widely than most of my instructors. The "bunk" in education bored me. Twittering about squirrels and birds, sentimentalizing over flowers, being sweet over nothing—this was nature study. I worked at mathematics and Latin and helped my fellow-students creep out of the dormitory. I did not myself steal out because it was not exciting enough in comparison with the life of intrigue against social pressure that I always led. One dormitory head was not nearly so hard to manage as were the several persons I had always heretofore needed to build defenses against.

When, at last a responsible person, I was teaching school away from home, life was less zestful and thrilling than in my parents' house. Here were no rules to break. I played cards gladly for one winter and have since then found them boresome. Dancing and flirting charmed me then and do still, but then as now I regarded them as trifles, not essentials. I was unmotivated and, except when I worked and played myself weary, a little unhappy. What was life for? Where was beauty? Where significance? I wanted children, but not marriage. I wanted men about me who were like my father, but more patient. I attract and like rascals, but villainy is not enough.

I taught for a while in the State Normal School from which I had graduated. The head of the English department got $1,500 a year for teaching two classes, while I got $900 for teaching four. He read, he boasted, nothing since Carlyle and Emerson. Between classes he raised pigs, played politics, grew rich. I liked Meredith, Henry James, Ibsen, Shaw, and wanted to stir students minds with them, but I had too little influence against my chief's inertia, partly because I was a young woman, and partly because I had no degree. Presumably more education would mean more salary, too. I hied me to college, after borrowing money from a stranger.

Life at the reputedly heretical university that I chose was useful. Sociology met needs in my mental make-up. Service as interpreted by sociology had meaning for me that organized religion never had. Suffrage enthusiasm was pleasing to me, but only the enthusiasm was unusual. I belonged at sight to all the liberal thought in the atmosphere. I observed girls getting with delight what I had been brought up on. Sex, which we read about, talked about, studied about, was absorbing, but the frank and sensible modern reaction to it was not startling to me. I was indignant when my attitude toward it shocked listeners.

I returned to teaching and to social work with a purposefulness that I had not before had. Joining the Women's Trade Union League and the Teachers' Union brought me into touch with organized labor. This contact has captivated me and held me. Like everything else that I have gone in for it is not enough, but I can find nothing better or more fundamental in our national life to which I can be attached.

I have run for office unsuccessfully on a progressive ticket. I am used to being punished for being a woman, a progressive, a scientifically minded educator, and, most of all, a person aware of corruption and graft.

I feel no need for more freedom, but I want a world in which the freedom I now have can be used. We women are free, but free for what? I move from disillusionment to fresh illusions. To be free makes life what it has always been, enticing. But my adventurous and questing mind was never so thwarted as it has been since I got my citizenship. The industrial and political world is in hands like mine today. Are we, while I live, going to get courage and wisdom to match our freedom? I am hopeful that we shall, but I suspect that I shall be disappointed as usual.

GARLAND SMITH

The Nation identifies the author of this essay as Garland Smith, but her name is all that has survived about her. She writes eloquently about the sexual anxieties of her southern Presbyterian girlhood, her fear of blasphemy, and the "vague subconscious impression that love, marriage, motherhood—everything remotely connected with sex—were considered vile." Smith managed to escape this environment for one year and go to New York to study at the Woman's Art School, a branch of Cooper Union which offered free classes. But the rigid curriculum depressed her; she returned home in defeat. For Smith, as for Lorine Pruette and Phyllis Blanchard and many other women of the period, the new psychology opened up genuine possibilities in life; such optimism as she expresses in her essay comes from her determined reading in G. Stanley Hall, Havelock Ellis, and Freud. Hall, a psychologist who pioneered the child-study movement, brought Freud and Jung to lecture at Clark University in Worcester, Massachusetts, where Hall later became president. He was not a feminist, but his writings on sexuality emphasized its normalcy. His most famous book, *Adolescence* (1904), repeated many Victorian beliefs about girls and women, but also gave a systematic portrayal of the turmoil, transition, and sexual awakening of adolescence. This book, and the work which it engendered, helped many women like Garland Smith to understand and accept their sexual feelings.

The Unpardonable Sin

I was born into an atmosphere of Presbyterian orthodoxy and conventionality, in a small Southern town—a biological "sport" in some ways; yet inheriting from my mother so much docility and from my father such a strain of introspection and over-conscientiousness that the best years of my life were wrecked.

That was before the days of ubiquitous psychology and child-study. Nobody had ever heard of such matters as complexes and repressions and maladjustments. The question of the psychical aspects of sex was untouched, it seems, except by a few foreign specialists. Afraid to be myself, afraid even to mention things I longed for most if I thought those things were disapproved of by the people around me, an exaggerated fearfulness held me captive. Some of its manifestations were so marked that it is hard to see how any grown person could have missed their significance. But these danger-signals my parents strangely ignored.

The fear of lying made me say "Maybe so and maybe not," in answer to questions. The fear of disobeying made me try to pinch a red ring around my leg one day when I went wading in a creek, so that I would not step in beyond the limit set by my mother. The fear of being sinful in vague, inexplicable ways oppressed me with a sense of guilt because a little boy kissed me in a game at a party when I was eight. That kiss worried me so that I was driven to confess the deed to my mother—not in a casual childish way but with a true Presbyterian sense of sin. There were other fears, including an absurd terror (at about five) of policemen: my eyes would fill with tears from fright at seeing one suddenly in the street.

Then at eleven the words "There is no God" flashed before my mind one day while I was studying my Sunday-school lesson, and I was filled with terror over being an atheist—"infidel," I called it. I thought I was a monster of wickedness because I could not believe in a God. But I simply could not, after those words appearing to my mind's eye. I would pray night and morning: "O God, let me believe!" I would stand before mirrors and study my face to see if the guilt of being an infidel had not marked it in some sinister way. I had heard of the mark of Cain, and I think I expected to find on my own countenance some mysterious sign that I was not like other people.

I still went regularly to church and Sunday school, and of course I dared not speak of my strange sin. I suffered in silence for about two years—less keenly as time passed—and then one day at Sunday school a new, inexpressible terror was shot at me by my teacher in the form of an explanation of the "unpardonable sin." There was one sin that could never be forgiven, she said—blasphemy against the Holy Ghost. She quoted from the Bible: "If a man blaspheme against the Son it shall be forgiven him; but if he blaspheme against the Holy Ghost he shall never be forgiven, but is in danger of everlasting fire." That woman is dead now. She left as a monument of herself a compilation of Bible texts called "Sunshine on Life's Path."

It is hard to give any idea to a healthy-minded person of the effect that statement had upon my sick little soul, at thirteen—of the insane terror of committing that sin in my thoughts at any minute. There might be a God—there must be—even though I could not actually believe in Him. And the thought: "If there is a God, if there is such a sin," engulfed me. The idea of blasphemy against the Holy Ghost and my terror produced a veritable obsession of insulting words and phrases such as I had never dreamed of saying in my life. And the more I repelled these "temptations," the more they thronged upon me. Every waking hour of my life I had to undergo the strain of banishing the suggestions of "blasphemy" that kept flocking into my mind; I had to be on my guard against them; had to counteract them by contradictory words or phrases and, as time went on, by jerks and motions of my body. Strange to say, I didn't go crazy. I was even considered brilliant at school, and was passionately fond of reading.

I began, after a year or so, to feel a wistful longing to be like other girls—to know boys, as they did, and go to parties and dances. There were not many parties for children in our little town, and it never occurred to my mother to have one for me. When I was twelve a "dancing party" was given by a girl a year or two older, and I was not invited. I heard my mother explain this slight to my father by saying "She doesn't dance, you know." She said to me years later, when I reproached her for my upbringing, that she had never wanted to dance when she was a girl, and never dreamed that I would care for it. She herself deeply disapproved of "round dances."

I cared for dancing intensely, having rhythm and poetry and romance in my very marrow. And of course in a college town, as mine was, a girl who does not dance is left out of nearly everything. As I was never invited to dances, I had literally no opportunity to meet boys. I went to a private school for girls only. If I walked home from school with a group of girls, I had to listen as they talked about their beaux and dances and fraternity pins, about this college boy and that, and I felt an aching loneliness that could not have been worse if I had been actually branded and cast out from human society.

If I happened to pass one of the few town boys in the street whom I had known when we were children I dared not look at him because I thought everyone despised and scorned me. Then I would go home and cry. By the time I was fifteen I had a well-developed sense of inferiority. I could not have spoken voluntarily to my mother about my loneliness and she never questioned me about my thoughts and feelings.

When I was about eleven, I heard her talk one day with other women about certain girls of fourteen or fifteen who "had boys in their heads," who were "boy crazy." Those expressions were burned into my memory, and the contempt and blame with which those girls seemed to be regarded. I got the idea that my mother considered it shameful, or at least unspeakably silly, for a girl ever to think about boys, ever to care to have boy friends.

All this time the "unpardonable-sin" horror was wearing out my nerves. I think I could have thrown it off if I had had the friends and diversion I longed for so intensely. But nobody seemed to suspect that I was not perfectly contented to stay at home and read, or draw and paint. Not my mother, not one of my numerous aunts, not one of my mother's women friends: nobody held out a hand to draw me into the circle of happy, normal girlhood. Instead, when I was not quite sixteen I had the misfortune to visit in the home of a sister-in-law of my father's, a sensational, stupid, vulgar woman, who, by her abnormal attitude toward sex, provided one more subject for introspection and worry and created another genuine complex: a vague, subconscious impression that love, marriage, motherhood—everything remotely connected with sex—were considered vile.

I fell in love at eighteen, when I finally had a chance to meet a boy. (A new family had moved to town, and lived in our neighborhood.) I didn't call it love. Being in love meant that you wanted to marry a person, and that was disgusting. But you might adore someone, much as saints adore their God. You might have an "ideal friendship" with someone who embodied the qualities you most admired. One heavenly conversation, the first time I talked to my idol; after that, dumbness and awkwardness in his presence. An inferiority complex is not to be thrown off all at once. Even when his sister said to me: "You've made a great impression on my brother. He thinks you are one of the nicest girls in this town," I could think of nothing to say.

I had finished school—the most advanced school in town—and there was no money for college. Nothing for me but to stay at home as always. No opportunities to meet boys and acquire social ease. Nothing going on in town but college dances, and a girl cannot go to dances without being invited. It still had not occurred to my mother that I might like to be introduced to a few boys and have a chance for the social life that I was secretly dying for, and I could not even hint at such a thing. So I read poetry and George Eliot and literary criticism and smatterings of philosophy and metaphysics, and wrote introspective outpourings in a journal that I kept fitfully. I wondered sometimes whether it were wrong to adore anybody as much as I adored my hero (I worshiped him steadily for ten years) even with no thought of "being in love." I wrote in my journal at nineteen: "Was it sentimentality, was it morbidness, was it merely the romanticism of youth finding vent in one accustomed to nothing but timorous self-repression?"

At twenty I went to New York to study "art." I knew nothing about the schools in New York except that one of them—a Woman's Art School— was free. So I selected that. I expected to enter the illustration class to get the technique for a profession with which to make a living. Then I was to paint landscapes. I had great notions of interpreting the beauty and poetry of nature, which I worshiped to the point of ecstasy. The curator of the school, a severe and stolid spinster, would not hear of my going into the illustration class. Thoroughness was her fetish. It was the "elementary antique," or nothing, the first year. And I was too incapable of self-assertion then to rebel. Thus the only year in which I ever had enough money to stay and study in New York was worse than wasted. It was literally soul-deadening to me to drudge for four hours a day at those ghastly casts.

I am at least free now from the old distortions and repressions. Beginning with Stanley Hall's "Adolescence," and going on through Freud and Brill and parts of Havelock Ellis and numerous other authors of these frank days, I have read enough to cure one of any amount of Puritanism. I am still an incorrigible idealist, however. And I still expect to "get started." The words of another idealist kept cropping up in my mind: "Yet I know all the while that I have never been defeated; have never yet fought, because I have never been weaponed for the fight; shall fight some day, when my hour comes, and shall win."

16

CORNELIA BRYCE PINCHOT

Cornelia Bryce Pinchot (1881-1960) was a 1920s version of the 1960s "superwoman," the woman who believes she must excel in her traditional feminine role as well as in a new professional role. Pinchot believed that "woman can bear children, charm her lovers, boss a business, swim the Channel, stand at Armegeddon and battle for the Lord—all in the day's work!" Of all the Nation women, only she had achieved her major distinction through marriage; her husband was Gifford Pinchot, the liberal Republican governor of Pennsylvania.

Born in Newport, Rhode Island, to a wealthy and prominent family, "Lelia" was educated in private schools. Beautiful and vivacious, she rebelled against the social conventions her family wished her to observe, enjoyed competitive sports, traveled, and steadily refused the offers of marriage which came to her. She was thirty-three when she married Pinchot in 1914. The marriage allowed her many opportunities to use her social and intellectual skills and to pursue her own political interests. According to one of Gifford Pinchot's biographers, she was "equally at home on a picket line with striking workers or as a lovely and gracious hostess at a formal reception." The fears of some Republicans that she might try to compete with her husband were allayed when she proved to be a strong and loyal campaigner who gave her energy—and her money—to his career. *The New York Times* wrote of their wedding: "Mrs. Gifford Pinchot will spend her honeymoon in working for her husband's election." She herself ran unsuccessfully three times for a seat in the House of Representatives in the 1920s.

Describing a life of unqualified ease and opportunity, in which even before suffrage she had never felt "downtrodden and disenfranchised," Pinchot is exuberantly optimistic about the "games" and "adventures" of women's lives. She does recognize how much would have to change before "average" women might even win economic independence; but overall she does not seem to have understood that her vision of feminism was well beyond the realities of life even for privileged women.

In Search of Adventure

An attempt to recreate the emotions or the facts of childhood is never easy; for almost everyone it must involve a certain amount of what comes perilously near to being sheer invention.

In my own case the child that was is dim to the woman that is. I can see, as through an inverted telescope, a series of microscopic pictures; a tiny tow-headed figure (two of them in fact, my sister and myself, one almost as detached as the other) moving about a background that shifts between New York, Washington, England, Newport, Long Island, France, and so on. The one that was me always in violent motion, full of spirits and eagerness, with a full measure of the adventures and rebellions, the joys and despairs that make up a thoroughly normal childhood.

Ironically enough, in view of my present interests, I was born at Newport in the early eighties. The earliest of my childish memories concerns a room, a strange, immense, unexpected room, with walls that did not behave as walls should, and a ceiling that was somehow "funny." It is curious how vivid it all remains—especially a hard, bright light and a smell which I have later identified as that of oil paints. A huge portrait still exists of my sister and myself, all fat legs and blue bows, painted by the leading Academician of the day. So probably the memory is of the studio in Rome where the horror was perpetrated, when I was somewhat under two years old.

Another picture, this time a steamer: a low quiet light; the sea still and glassy; myself on deck peering between the rails over which I was too small to see; rows of comfortable ladies on deck chairs consuming tea and taffy, that sweet, sticky stuff provided, thanks be to Heaven, only on Cunarders; everywhere peace and serenity. Suddenly a grinding shock, a shiver through the ship, a grating, wrenching, jerking forward for several seconds, and finally a bump that brought us all to our feet. Then somehow in everybody's mouth the mysterious words, "We're aground." I knew exactly what to expect—a raft, desert island, monkeys, a house in a palm tree, all in the best Crusoe tradition. This in spite of the fact that the shores of Staten Island were still faintly visible in the haze. For the first time I tasted to the full the bitterness of disillusion. I can remember as if it were yesterday the first dreadful doubts that sprang to my mind as I realized that my mother, who had never failed me before, was sitting calmly in her chair, that no joyful activities were on foot, no lashing together of masts to make rafts, no gathering up of water-kegs and axes and all the other delightful paraphernalia of adventure, as I had so confidently anticipated. Something very close to despair filled my soul as it was finally borne in upon me that my island was but a mirage, that dull ships would go on forever sailing to duller destinations. The taste of taffy brings it all back to me, even to the disintegrating nausea of the piece tucked in my cheek throughout the excitement—the piece I spat fiercely into the sea with a feeling that somehow the doors of life had clanged shut upon romance.

This anticlimax was all the more devastating as I had been frankly "scared." It was not until many years later that I realized what a joyful, soul-satisfying sensation the word implies. Always the same rhythm—first an overpowering oppression, a tight clutch at one's throat almost like a physical bond, then the revulsion: a sudden, soaring, wide-flung feeling of delight, of tremendous possibilities just ahead, an intoxicating illusion of sudden power. A sensation to be prized above all others and to be courted in all manner of ways. It is much the same today—whether the occasion be the stalling of an airplane engine low over London, picketing surrounded by a crowd of angry scabs, swimming among sharks, the schooling of a green hunter.

Even careening down a steep hill with a drunken taxi-driver, his machine out of control, has its points.

Intense physical pain has a similar effect. After the first oppression, the first grinding annihilation, comes the same revulsion, the same fierce release of the spirit, the same sense of swinging incredibly free above the limitations of an everyday world. Ever since my first child was born, I have known that one day the world's supreme work of art would be created by a woman in childbirth.

But to return to my commonplace and uneventful childhood. Another memory: a calm windless afternoon, a golden sunset—and my pet rabbit, its leg crushed by my clumsiness. The agony of that moment will have power to torture me till the end of my life. After all these years I still waken in a cold sweat, the feel of the soft little body under my foot, its screams ringing through the room.

The scene shifts to a London hotel—my mother, in a dress of flame, coming in to tell us goodnight. I remember my feeling of stunned consternation as I realized she was dining out *in England!* Actually about to break bread with *the British enemy!* It seemed an act of unutterable treachery impossible to understand. Obviously the propaganda then fed to the young under the guise of patriotism had borne its fruits.

One more story and I am done. Since I had read "Ben Hur" at the age of six, a small white birthmark on my breast assumed a new interest and was immediately identified as the mark of incipient leprosy. With a feeling part disgust, part triumph, part excitement, I rode into the park on my little old tricycle, debating seriously with myself whether I must not shout "Unclean!" "Unclean!" to the children that rushed up to greet me, and then steal quietly away into the mountains of Palestine. But of course never a sign of all this to parents, governesses, nurses, or indeed to anyone. I would have died before letting a word of it pass my lips.

Commonplace as are these incidents of my childhood, the next phase is even more undramatic. The stage was set for a conventional coming-out, and the normal sequellae to be expected from the daughter of my sort of parents—none of which happened. My father and mother, much to their surprise, were forced to adjust themselves to a "dud" in the family circle. I don't know how seriously they took it, but I do know that life was made uncomfortable for me through an atmosphere of failure, of having somehow not to come up to expectations, so much so that I went around with a sense of guilt and rather bitter revolt.

I flatly refused to "come out," but I had not the faintest idea what I did want. I only knew that I was "agin" everything the family wanted —all its traditions, all its theories, all its works. This sense of revolt— my hand against every man, especially against the rich and established —may have come from something more deeprooted than the ordinary rebellion of the young against their parents; I don't know, but at any rate, it is even now a fundamental part of my make-up. Some years ago my husband and I were forced to endure several months of intensive police protection. Over and beyond the inevitable nuisance of having a secret-service man at one's elbow morning, noon, and night, was a feeling of resentment, of being in a humiliating position. I had always the sense that the police were the natural enemy, that they and I belonged to different camps. No amount of reasoning could overcome the sensation. I experienced much the same discomfort on my first visit to a steel mill, where even "tapping a heat" for the first time—one of the real thrills of my life—could not make me unconscious of the obsequious manager who trailed us from shop to shop, giving me the same humiliating sense of sailing under false colors. What had I to do with the Steel Trust or any of its works?

However, in spite of revolts and rebellions, I managed to have an extremely good time. For several of those years I went in heavily for sports—one in particular with a reputation for danger (in which women rarely competed) affording a most gratifying opportunity to score against hard-boiled masculine competition.

The inevitable young men turned up at times in considerable numbers. I was sent the other day an old letter of my mother's that complained of three diamond solitaires found in a discarded bureau about which, according to her, I professed to have no interest—but flippantly suggested that she attempt to return them to the young men in question, and see whether she might be more successful than I. Her disgust with my behavior, her reluctance to give the offending articles houseroom in her safe, combined with her inability to leave them where she found them, served to illustrate the difference between the two generations. Incidentally, I have not the slightest recollection of the occurrence.

Then one fine day I made up my mind to shed my present and my past—decided to go out and see the world from a new angle. With a portentous feeling as of one signing a declaration of independence I discarded both my pearls and my maid and, having provided myself with letters of introduction to all the great, the near-great, and the not great at all from Maine to California, I started out with a wise friend. For the first time in my life I was foot-loose—with no family to consider or demonstrate against. We would arrive in a town, having sent our letters ahead, to find a welcome arranged for us by the leading citizens perhaps, or by a puzzled mayor—both quite uncertain whether they were to deal with lady adventuresses, uplifters, or a new brand of drummer. One of my most cherished possessions is a card from a bell-hop in a Los Angeles hotel to his friend in San Francisco, tenderly inscribed: "Be good to these girls." As a pendant to this story was a perfectly impersonal, almost public proposal of marriage, after a few hours' acquaintance, by a tory statesman, very rich and pompous, evidently because he felt it was expected of him. We had all manner of joyful adventures and collected I.W.W.'s, big-game hunters, reactionary Senators, Socialists, stodgy captains of industries, single taxers, a whole-hog Tolstoian, college professors, and editors galore—even a Hindu agitator. It was a good trip and things began to move from then on.

I cannot remember just when or how I first became interested in the suffrage movement—but I do know that it came more through my active interest in liberal politics than through the usual resentment against women's political discrimination per se. Many of my family had held elective offices of one kind and another. I remember more than once dining with an ex-President who took me into the smoking-room to talk politics with the men after the women had left the table, and it never struck me that this was in any way unusual. I had not learned to think of myself in terms of a downtrodden and disfranchised female.

I walked in the first suffrage parade and in some later ones as a matter of course and without feeling that I was doing anything significant. My family were opposed, equally as a matter of course, but I cannot remember that that particular bone of contention was ever seriously worried between us. As time went on, I joined actively in the suffrage fight and gave considerable time to it, but I must admit that quite aside from the essential justice of the proposition, I saw women largely as a new group of voters. I worked to help enfranchise them with even more interest in their responsibilities than in their rights.

Since then, in the language of the booster, more adventures and better adventures have come into my life—some successes, some reverses—but no more negations, no further futilities. Some years ago I marked down, pursued, and captured one of the few really big men I have ever known—"one who never turned his back but marched breast forward"—and lived happily and gloriously ever after.

My interests have continued to be specialized along actively political lines. My feminism has broadened and become more human, more understanding, especially in my belated recognition of the vital importance of economic independence for women, and the need of constructive action to make that possible for the average wife and mother.

On one point, however, I take direct issue with orthodox feminists, many of whom assume that the bearing of children is a burden and a handicap, and that men's exemption therefrom constitutes an asset. I disagree. In the first place many women tend to over-emphasize the question of physical pain; and in the second, even if one admits that the adventure of child-bearing "gums the game" for a certain period, there is no reason for assuming that this in itself constitutes a cost too high to be borne with eager, glorying equanimity; nor that because he is free from it man has essentially the better part. Personally I would not change, abate, or sacrifice any part of my own job.

My feminism tells me that woman can bear children, charm her lovers, boss a business, swim the Channel, stand at Armageddon and battle for the Lord—all in the day's work!

17

WANDA GAG

Wanda Gág (1893-1946), an artist and children's book writer, grew up in the village of New Ulm, Minnesota. When her father died of tuberculosis and her mother also contracted the disease, fifteen-year-old Wanda, the oldest of the seven Gág children, became the dominant force in the family. It was she who decided that all the children should finish school, and she helped support them by giving art lessons, making and selling greeting cards, and writing short pieces for the local newspaper. After high school, Gág won a series of scholarships to art schools, first in

Minnesota, and in 1917, at the Art Students League in New York. By the mid-1920s, she had begun to achieve recognition through shows at the New York Public Library and the Weyhe Gallery. Later she became well-known and prosperous through her children's books, and her illustrations for *Tales from Grimm* (1936). In 1930, she bought a large farm in New Jersey, where she lived for the rest of her life with her husband, Earle Marshall Humphreys, and her brother and youngest sister. Gág died of lung cancer at the age of fifty-three.

In her essay, Gág turns her difficult and impoverished childhood into a gay adventure, making hunger and shabbiness sound like *Little Women*. Like Genevieve Taggard's family, the Gágs (like the Muhrs of the essay) took pride in being different from the natives of their dull, respectable small town. To be an artist and not a "New Swabian" became Gág's sustaining goal. Her greatest difficulties, as she presents them here, were personal. Once in New York, she did not find it difficult to meet men who would accept her ambitions and agree to share household responsibilities —up to a point. But she could not see how the kind of life she wanted for herself could include children, as much as she wanted them. The strongest feelings expressed in her essay are about her realization that she would have to choose between creating aesthetically and creating physically. Gág reports with pleasure that the men she met in New York raised no objections to her decision not to have children and, in fact, "seemed to prefer this attitude in women." She does not seem to have thought very seriously about the injustice of having to choose, or to have blamed anything but "good old Mother Nature" for her problems. But it is interesting to note that when Gág "drew up an outline for a contract marriage," she never even showed it to the man she wanted to marry. Her story gives us some indication of the kinds of stresses created when the changes in women's expectations and roles are not matched by changes in men.

A Hotbed of Feminists

A vague smell of olive oil and mama in bed—this combination always meant a new baby.

In our family it was one girl after another, which pleased me greatly, for I considered boys not only unaesthetic but extremely unnecessary creatures. Not so my father! Though fond and proud of his collection of incipient artists (they all drew as soon as they could hold a pencil), he was always a little piqued at the non-appearance of a son.

The sixth venture brought the desired result. A boy at last—a Muhr who would stay Muhr through all the mutabilities of life and marriage! I remember father on the night of this event—running busily up and down the stairs, his face swollen with toothache, but radiant with ineffable joy and triumph. Now his family was complete!

My father was too idealistic to face the fact that no artist could survive in a mediocre Middle Western village. True, New Swabia had a rich European background and a sturdy pioneer past, but the vitiating spirit of Main Street was already becoming evident, and after all that was what father had to combat.

He painted and decorated houses for a living and kept us in modest comfort. On Sundays he painted pictures in our attic *Malzimmer*. My mother, and even the half-peasant uncles and aunts "down at grandma's" had the aesthetic urge in some form or other—and I spent my earliest years in the serene belief that drawing and painting, like eating and sleeping, belonged to the universal and inevitable things of life.

My mother, who was a natural iconoclast, arranged our hair in unusual ways, refused to burden us with starched clothes, and considered shoes and stocking unnecessary in hot weather, Sundays included. Our Sundays were *gemütlich:* The mingled smell of paints and a Sunday cigar drifting down from the Malzimmer, *Zimmtkuchen* in the kitchen, and Sabbath chimes floating in to us from five directions. The latter gave us a vicarious feeling of sanctity, for we never went to church. We were not even christened. My parents, both Catholic Bohemians by birth, had deserted their faith in early youth and were now "nothing," as I was often forced to admit to my playmates. These children, safe in the folds of some church or other, informed me of our unfitness for heaven. I asked my father about it, and he said: "Nobody knows what will happen to us. Just do the best you know how and everything will be all right."

Somehow, we got away with all this. "It's all very well for the Muhrs," said the people, "because they're artist's children."

I had always regarded my father's delicate constitution as something which went with his being an artist, much like his long slender fingers or his pointed beard. But as time went on, it could not be passed off in so romantic a fashion. It was easy to see that he was worried about it, too, and to make matters worse, after four years another child was born—a girl! Father was not much pleased. While mama was having the baby, he was in a neighboring town painting murals in a damp, unheated church. When he returned, he was forced to stop working and put to bed. On the baby's first birthday he was buried.

We felt dazed and helpless. Father had been unable to work during that last year—all we had was the house and his insurance amounting to a thousand dollars. "You'll have to take in washing," mother was told, "and Senta, of course, must clerk in a store and support the family." But mother, after the strain of the past year, was too weary and ill to do even her own housework, and I could see that the few dollars I would earn as a clerk in a village store would never solve our problem. Besides I was needed at home to help with the housework and to take care of the baby. This I did, and by drawing place-cards and writing childrens' stories which I illustrated I earned about as much as the store job would have brought.

There followed years of struggle for us all. To me it was a jumble of housework, hungry children, endless wood-chopping, "drawing-fits," and adolescent sentimental moods—and a yearning for oysters and butter.

We determined that the title of the house should be kept clear and that we were never to get into debt. The insurance money was made to stretch over six years, so even with occasional donations, and eight dollars a month which the county allowed us for groceries, there was rarely enough food. Our meals were often pitiful—in retrospect, amusingly so. For instance there was the famous "Dingle supper." Dingle was an old baker who sold us stale sugarrolls—having a rancid taste—very cheap. A dime bought enough of these for a scanty supper, the sugar coating serving as a substitute for molasses—butter and jelly were to us the rarest luxuries. We ate Dingle rolls and nothing else.

It was a task to divide the food fairly between us, until we thought of putting it on the basis of a game of chance. After making seven equal divisions (mother always took a smaller share with the excuse that she was not growing any more), one of us numbered the portions mentally. Each child chose a number at random, and received the portion which that number represented. As there was no finding fault with one's choice, everybody had to be satisfied. It might be supposed that the one who did the numbering could juggle the portions to her advantage, but no one thought of questioning her integrity. There is no way in which I can describe our extreme sense of honor in this matter, swearing on the Bible being a pale oath by comparison.

Among the donations we rejoiced in were other people's cast-off clothes. I often went blocks out of my way to avoid meeting the person whose contribution I happened to be wearing. We soon learned to remodel them beyond recognition, and became so expert that we were criticized for "dressing so swell." I could not stop drawing and reading and was made to feel guilty for that. "Senta could find something better to do than sit in the yard and read and draw all the time." We were finally completely crushed by these criticisms and regained our self-respect only when we were safely assembled in our funny tall house, where we drew, sang, and played games among ourselves. I think this self-sufficiency, in spite of our poverty, nettled the New Swabians.

After a year and a half at home I came, not without tears and fumbling, to an important conclusion. Things were looking hopeless, and it seemed to me that whether we were to swim and come out Muhrs, or sink and stay New Swabians forever, depended on a plunge —a high-school education for us all. To have planned this for the rest and sacrificed myself to the noble cause would have been preposterous enough in the eyes of the natives; but brazenly to include myself was nothing short of selfish; and it was, in a way. I was eager to help the family, to be sure, but how much of me did they really need—all? How much did I belong to myself? To what extent had I the right to ignore myself—not the physical part that walked around and worked, but that fiery thing inside which was always trying to get out and which made me draw so furiously? That was something to be considered, too. Hadn't papa told me? His last conscious words had been in regard to this very thing. "Senta," he had said faintly and with that utter-artist look in his eyes, "what papa has left undone, you'll have to do." And I had nodded my head, speechless with the sudden realization that he was dying and overwhelmed with the poignant drama of what was happening to me.

Now then, was not this a justification of my course? It was more than that—a rich legacy, a coat of mail, something to fight the world with! A defiance flashed into birth within me, "I must go to school again!" Mother was willing if I could see a way to do it. A few discerning people saw my point of view and even offered to help me. And so I went to high school, earning more than my way by drawing and writing stories as before, and giving many a day besides to household duties.

After graduating I taught country school for a year. The autumn after that, my oldest sister Barbara was ready to teach, which was fortunate, for in the meantime I had won a scholarship and was sent away to art school—not by the New Swabians, and not without the usual hints as to my selfishness from some of them. One favorite criticism was: "Why didn't she go on teaching school? Here she went and got a good education, and all for nothing!"

Art school brought cavaliers and the question of marriage. With my father as an example of one who had tried to combine art and a family (and with his family still on my hands!) I hesitated. My drawing fits were my greatest joy; and much as I liked men, I knew that art would always have to come first. I made the startling announcement that I would marry no man unless he would promise to run the house during my drawing moods and would excuse me from scrubbing floors. At the Y. W., where I was staying, the girls were horrified at my "unwomanly attitude" and thought I would make an unnatural wife. But the boys at school were merely amused, probably because they thought I would forget all about it when I found the right man.

During the next several years I had the good fortune to find another patron. I managed also to get friendly contributions for the family from various sources. Erda, the third Muhr, had just started teaching when our weary mother, who had been fading away before our eyes all these years, died. We must have looked as forlorn as we felt, for people really seemed to feel sorry for us. The children were well-behaved and rather pretty, and several childless couples offered to adopt them and give them "good homes." This would have simplified matters considerably but I could not accept—for, although the term "bourgeois" was not in my vocabulary at the time, I felt its meaning instinctively and revolted against it.

Then there were the Methodists who had long had a missionary eye on us and who finally saw a chance of rescuing the youngsters from my heathen clutches. In order to soften me toward their plan of taking the three youngest to their orphan asylum, they voted us five dollars' worth of groceries. I withheld my negative answer until the food was safely in my hands, my ethics at that desperate stage being that of the proverbial lioness and her cubs.

Instead of thus giving the children a chance to grow up in comfort I made a plan, precarious perhaps, but in my estimation not as "crazy" as people told me it was. I sold the house and moved the family to a big city. The children were delighted and said they would gladly put up with anything to get to a place where our poverty would not be known. We decided to use the house-money for rent, light, and fuel during the next six years. I, who was about to be sent East on another scholarship, would send what I could. Barbara and Erda, since they were escaping room rent by this plan, would take care of the food and clothing. The fourth Muhr, just finishing school, would keep house; and Erda, who had a knack for such things, would manage the family budget.

After coming to New York, I went through a long and agonized period of disillusionment. One fact after another was pushed down my throat, and it seemed as though I would never get through swallowing. The fact that one of my youthful love affairs was running into a somewhat sterner phase only bewildered me the more. What was one going to do about it? Homer, an incipient radical, was as shy of marriage as I was. Free love? The idea did not shock me, but it was hardly a solution if one planned to have babies.

Both courses seemed so extreme—was there no happy medium? With my room-mate's help I drew up an outline for a contract marriage, but I never even showed it to Homer and our problem remained unsolved. However, I lost no opportunity after that of asking the advice of almost everybody I met. Since most of these were men, I soon found myself in possession of an exceedingly liberal education in regard to men, women, and sex.

I pondered and wept over my new information, but there was no getting around it; "good old Mother Nature" was merciless, selfish, and deceitful—and above all, cruel to women. I began to wish I had been born a man. About the physical disadvantages of being a woman nothing could be done; but there were certain privileges which men possessed merely because of custom, and these it might be possible to capture and make one's own.

And babies? One day a well-known artist asked me what kind of drawings I was most interested in doing. I said promptly, "Children's illustrations."

"Oh," he said in mild disgust. "Women are always drawing children."

It made me a little angry; not so much with him as with myself. Was I just another one of those sentimentally maternal females? Why did I want children, anyway? Because I was interested in drawing and raising them, because I was curious to see what I would produce, and because I wanted to reinvest my aesthetic urge in another human being. And how did these reasons stack up against the one big urge to express myself in drawing and painting? This difficult debate with myself lasted for several years and ended with my conviction that if it came to a choice I was more interested in creating aesthetically than physically.

I am fond of men, and at first I was afraid that these new convictions might drive them away. In general, however, I was pleased to find that most of the men I met were not only willing to put up with but actually seemed to prefer this attitude in women.

Our family struggles are not over yet, but we have managed to keep afloat and, I believe, are coming out Muhrs. If papa had only known what a hotbed of feminists he was starting, he need not have worried so about having a boy; for, with one exception, all his daughters bid fair to remain Muhrs through all the mutabilities of life and marriage.

THE PSYCHOLOGISTS' RESPONSES

The *Nation* editors selected three well-known psychologists to respond to the "modern women" series, and their articles were printed under the heading "Explaining Women." Beatrice M. Hinkle, a feminist and a Jungian psychoanalyst, was the most sympathetic commentator, although she found the contributors "weak on their woman's nature." Both John M. Watson, an extreme behaviorist, and Joseph Collins, a neurologist, were very critical of the essayists.

Why Feminism?

BEATRICE M. HINKLE

The women who pictured their early backgrounds for *The Nation* in an effort to explain their later "feminist" behavior attempted the impossible. The incidents and general conditions of the environment that one consciously remembers, the external aspect of life, are but a part, indeed the smaller part, of one's background. Silently and quite apart from the will and knowledge of the child a mysterious alchemy takes place between the inherited reaction-trends, the dominant psychological functions of the particular individual, and the environmental influences which play upon them. Out of this welter arise the marked characteristics and attitudes which become organized in the mature personality.

We know that biologically two marked reactions to the same stimulus among living beings are always possible. For instance, fear produces the familiar fight-or-flight reaction; frequently, both reactions occur in the same individual, one following the other. Different individual organisms will react differently and unpredictably to the same condition or environment. Among human beings there are many choices of reaction to a specific stimulus or environmental situation but it is safe to say that the specific attitude taken is the only one possible to the individual at the time his general direction is being formed.

The inadequacy of attempting to explain the particular destiny of an individual solely by some special type of environment is amply attested by these women's stories. The tendency they show to consider their own lives as the direct result of their external environment is natural and common to most persons. However, what they most clearly reveal in varying degrees is the particularly personal character of their opinions and attitudes.

For example, in the first story we have the statement of the writer that she, "the most timid of created beings," was nevertheless an active participant in one fight after another and a feminist of the militant type. From the account of the family background it is evident that there was an atmosphere in the home of free discussion and a liberal attitude toward women's aspirations. There were women members of the household whose attitude was apparently distinctively modern, and therefore she imbibed during her youth the special nutriment which stimulated the individualistic aspect of her personality. Her exultation over the "first brick thrown" in the militant suffrage cause was a joyous release to action through the psychological mechanisms of identification with the thrower, for she was thus enabled to overcome her personal timidity through a collective action.

Even though these stories are inadequate for an analysis of the writers, due to their marked concern with family conditions and the obvious repression of any clear picture of the individual in the family, they do present conditions which inevitably play an important role in affecting the general attitude of the developing child.

The failure to present clear-cut individual personalities makes it necessary to consider these women as similar types because of their "feminist" opinions and a so-called modern attitude toward children, marriage, and jobs. Of course this is not true, for although the writers share a "modern" point of view they have no general, common attitude. For instance, the woman who has not married and who states that she regards marriage as a compromise is a very different person from the one who finds herself comfortably married with the feeling that it is good, and that neither economic dependence or independence makes much difference. Nevertheless, when attempting to consider a group of different personalities, nothing more than a collective survey can be made.

Two distinct types of family environment are described in these histories and are highly important in their influence on the children. In one group there is a distinctly feminist and free attitude on the part of the parents and close relatives. There are play of ideas, free discussion, and equality between the boys and girls in the family. The children were surrounded by this atmosphere from birth, and accordingly their intellectual espousal of the feminist cause was a natural development, an acceptance of the family attitude, and not something born out of personal revolt.

Such a case is the one described as Mother-Worship. Here the girl had a constant example before her in the harmonious attitude of both parents toward sex equality and in their freedom from ordinary conventions, besides the actual experience of the mother's unusual life activities. To be sure this same condition might have produced an opposite reaction in another type of child, but not where so strong an admiration and love for the mother existed, coupled with mother-identification. There is no evidence that this woman's modern attitude was born of revolt or included a protest at all. It was a natural, an easy (perhaps too easy, as she herself comments), acceptance of the general family attitude and thought. The same can be said of the writers of the stories, Staying Free and Lightning Speed Through Life. Their efforts in the world cannot be said to be of a different nature than those of any man who wishes to achieve the fulfilment of his ideas, and struggles to carry on his activities on that basis. In other words, the feminism of these women was not born out of a sense of injustice and bitterness, but developed as a natural growth from their own personality in contact with the special family environment. On the other hand, this same environment might well be conceived to be the cause of a violent revolt when the young women went into the world and found themselves hampered by the existing inequalities and traditional attitudes toward women.

Quite different is the second group. Here there are family conditions in which grinding poverty, conservative ideas, heavily burdened, unhappy mothers, and a serious responsible childhood prevail. The opinions and attitudes of these women are largely conditioned by revolt against the trying circumstances which they experienced. A fight reaction manifested itself in their protests against and overthrow of the conditions prevailing in their families. Like the first group, they were undoubtedly aided by the lessening of the social restriction of women still strong during the early life of their mothers.

All this represents one half of the problem. The other half is the type of the individual upon whom these influences fell. For we know that the same family conditions need not produce the same effect upon another type of child, and in these very families there are probably sisters who did not react as these writers did. The problem narrows down to this: What is the real inner cause of the revolt in the souls of these women?

Adler would probably account for their attitude by calling them victims of the masculine protest, and see their revolt as an expression of an organically determined inferiority complex which compensates itself by the espousal of the cause of women as a class, and by a refusal to accept the traditional submissive role.

The Freudian analyst would diagnose them as suffering from a castration complex and explain their revolt as an abnormal manifestation of an inner protest that they were not men; in other words, as a refusal to accept their own sex and live the love life of women. There does not appear to be much distinction between these two conceptions except as regards terminology and emphasis. Each authority postulates his thesis in the traditional conceptions of woman's psychology and position.

My own point of view is that, given their particular psychological organism with its need and capacity for change and development, together with the special family conditions and the comparatively free outer environment, their attitude is a normal protest against external collective restrictions. In the economic struggle women have been notoriously exploited and misused, and there is a definite analogy between their attitude of revolt and that of subject peoples and exploited workers of the male sex. It is significant that in not one of these cases is the feminism of the women based on principle but in each instance it was born directly from the necessities of their personal life.

The most common experience among these women is that of their later education and final goal. All but two were college-trained; all of necessity were self-supporting.

A striking revelation in these "backgrounds" is the overwhelming part played by the mother in the family and, in the majority of cases, in the lives of the daughters. It was the mother on whom many of the families depended for their economic existence and for the education of the children; it was the mother on whom the affection and respect of the daughters were focused. Even though in some of the mother-dominated families the father made an effort to assume economic responsibility, the mother continuously contributed her share to the exchequer. In the cases where the father is especially mentioned with love and preference by the daughter, the mother still remained the gallant figure in the economic life of the family. These mothers are largely of the pioneer type and they present unmistakably the basis for the external freedom and unusual position of importance possessed by women in general in this country.

Although our group of feminist women appear from their statements to have achieved some kind of fulfilment, it is obvious in spite of their concealments that they have not achieved an inner freedom, or a real solution of their personal problems. They are weak on the side of their woman's nature. Several of them are married, but children are few; and taking them as a group, the general deduction to be drawn is that the love life is meager and that little enrichment of the personalities through the love experience has been gained. Men might say that their unsatisfied sex impulses produce a vicarious activity manifesting itself in "unwomanly" feminist ideas. We can without difficulty agree that the sexual energy provides a driving power for this type of interest as it does for every form of creative activity. But no woman who has lived through such an experience will admit that bearing large families, exhausting energy in the painful economic struggle to support children, as did the mothers of these women, offers to the individual woman or to the race a more satisfactory way of life.

These modern women are engaged in a real creative effort even though it may not be realized, for behind their stridency and revolt lies the great inner meaning of woman's struggle with the forces of convention and inertia. This is nothing less than the psychological development of themselves as individuals, in contradistinction to the collective destiny that has exclusively dominated their lives.

In spite of their individual failure to achieve their full destiny—and who fulfils it to his complete satisfaction, whether man or woman?—their attitude is part of a great rolling tide which is bringing to birth a new woman. This new woman will possess an individuality which will enable her to stand by the side of man, strong and secure within herself. From her a new race will be born for whom feminism or masculine antagonism will be but an echo of a dark age long past.

The Weakness of Women

JOHN B. WATSON

How much truth are the women telling in their biographies? At best biographies reveal mainly superficialities. It is curious that human beings know so little about themselves. We almost never tear ourselves apart to see how the parts work together. It is so much easier to tear other people apart. We learn from infancy to lay blame for failure upon parents, home life, associates, early economic conditions. If we win through it must be because of some innate, instinctive virtue in us that will not be downed by adversity. This all comes out in the biographies. One is struck by the failure on the part of almost all of the women to pay tribute to the very adversities of the environment. Nearly all of them actually quarreled with it—magnified its hardships. "What rot," says the behaviorist who believes that all individuals are made, not born, "the very sorrows and tribulations these women passed through were the conditioning stimuli which forced them on their way." Probably under what they would have considered a favorable environment most of them would have reached the age of fatness and forty and never been heard of—I speak freely, since I know none of the ladies.

The second thing that strikes one about these brief life histories is that the women were all restless—seeking something. What were they striving for—happiness? No, happiness apparently has gone out of fashion, it is not a present-day desideratum. We ask people today how many cars they have, whether they live in the town or the country or both, whether they play golf, tennis, or bridge, but we never ask whether they are happy or not. I doubt if very many children or adults today would understand what you meant if you did ask them, and I insist that happiness can be defined objectively in behavior terms, that it is a mode of behavior. These women were too modern to seek happiness; they sought what? Freedom. So many hundreds of women I have talked to have sought freedom. I have tried to find out diplomatically but behavioristically what they mean. Is it to wear trousers? Is it to vote—to hold office—to work at men's trades—to take men's jobs away from them—to get men's salaries? Does their demand for this mystical thing called freedom imply a resentment against child-bearing—a resentment against the fact that men's sex behavior is different from women's (but not so much any more)? I rarely arrive at a reasonable answer. The analysts claim that they can by psychoanalysis get at the truth about women. I make no such rash claim. I can read women only after making careful observations of their behavior over long periods of time. Then I put two and two together like any other scientist. When a woman is a militant suffragist the chances are, shall we say, a hundred to one that her sex life is not well adjusted? Marriage as such brings adjustment in only approximately 20 per cent of all cases, so poorly have men and women been taught about sex. Among the 20 per cent who find adjustment I find no militant women, I find no women shouting about their rights to some fanciful career that men—the brutes—have robbed them of. They work—they work like a man (than which nothing better can be said about work)—they often quietly achieve careers. Most of the terrible women one must meet, women with the blatant views and voices, women who have to be noticed, who shoulder one about, who can't take life quietly, belong to this large percentage of women who have never made a sex adjustment.

The biographies as a whole strikingly confirm the view that militancy passes as soon as the woman, by the trial-and-error process, finds sex adjustment. Then they cease to hunt for freedom, they lose themselves in their work. Surely the only freedom worth striving for is complete engrossment in activity, be that activity writing a play, washing infant's clothes, or losing oneself in the sway of passion.

The great weakness of women (who seek careers) is that they have never been trained to work like men. I mean trained so from infancy. Men are brought up in the tradition that men must work. They get it in their youth in gang activities and later in sports. They learn from boyhood that they must support their families and that to do so they must establish technique for work—habits of work—and that they must endure fatigue to harden their muscles; they must learn to do everything well enough to compete. They are trained in their infancy in habits of manipulation—women are not. They used to be in the fine art of needlework—only look at the samplers of the eight to twelve-year-olds. They were trained to weave and spin and cook and make their own dresses. Then the fashion changed—women had to be ladies— pretty ornaments. Their sphere was in the home. Now the picture is changing again. Mothers are beginning to train their girls in habits of manipulation. Women's customs have changed so rapidly that work traditions have never had a chance to soak in. Hence few women have achieved greatness.

I have never believed that there were any unsuperable difficulties which keep women from succeeding. They have strength enough to paint, yet there has never been a great woman painter. They have strength enough to play the violin and yet there has never been a great woman violinist. They have endurance and strength enough to become great scientists and yet one can count on fewer than the fingers of one hand the women scientists who have achieved real greatness. During the past thirty years thousands of women have taken the degree of Ph.D. and yet scarcely a dozen have come to the front.

Not being trained from infancy to the tradition of incessant manipulative work they drop out of the race as soon as they get comfortable. Marriage is usually the shady spot that causes them to lie down and rest. And when they fail in that, as 80 per cent do, restlessness again sets in, but now it is too late to go back and take up the threads of the old career. Most women who had aspirations for a career have tried to eat their cake and have it too. A career is a jealous all-consuming taskmaster.

Marriage as such should be no barrier to a career. Apartment hotels, which can be found in every town where a woman would have a career, have freed married women without children almost completely. The having of children is almost an insuperable barrier to a career. The rearing of children and the running of a home for them is a profession second to none in its demands for technique.

The behavioristic moral—and we must have morals—is: Women do not like to work (neither do men). There is no natural "instinct" to work. Biologically speaking the hungry animal reaches up and pulls down a banana, reaches out and grasps his female (or vice versa); his hunger adjusted, he rests and sleeps. Work habits are the result of civilization and competition. If you want your children to have careers, be they boys or girls, teach them from infancy habits of manipulation, skilful technique, endurance. Work must become "first nature"— "second nature" is not enough. And along with it teach them (or have them taught if you are a Puritan) what to expect in the realm of sex.

Half-Confessed

JOSEPH COLLINS

Articulate confession is better for the soul than scriptural. It is likewise better for the confessor seeking illumination of sin, sanity, or sanctity. The women who have been telling through *The Nation* why and how they rebelled against some of the conventions to which they were born and reared can scarcely have had the exquisite feeling of purity and spiritual lightness that comes from frank and full confession. They have kept back a lot, and no experienced confessor like myself will give them absolution.

The writers are all revolutionists; that is, they are all feminists. There are many varieties of feminists but they all have one thing in common: enmity to privilege. Feminists want to do something in the world and to do it themselves.

Privilege has always precipitated revolutions. Privileges that man arrogated to himself precipitated feminism. Had it not been for Paul, Luther, and Loyola women would have had their rights hundreds of years ago. Now that they have them in part, and soon are to have them in full measure, it behooves women to use them properly. I can see no sign that they are seeking or getting instruction in that direction. I have no doubt many echo the sentiment of the woman who wrote in *The Nation* series:

I feel no need for more freedom, but I want a world in which the freedom I now have can be used. The industrial and political world is in hands like mine today. Are we, while I live, going to get courage and wisdom to match our freedom? I am hopeful that we shall, but I suspect that I shall be disappointed.

The question that woman must answer is Why am I here? not Where am I at? Woman has one purpose: to help God run the world. In every respect save populating it, He would seem to be wholly beyond the need of assistance from His image. Until man began to sin, God had only one command: "Be fruitful and multiply; replenish the earth and subdue it." Woman is chiefly concerned with the first part of the command, man with the second. Incidentally, she may express herself, strive to be happy, and help make life livable for others. Those are privileges, not duties. Woman is becoming more and more loath to do her duty; man more and more eager to obey God's command. Flying over the Atlantic without stop, telephoning from London to San Francisco qualify under "subdue the earth." The woman who is willing to have ten to twenty children is almost extinct.

There are many good reasons why the majority of women should not have ten to twenty children, but there are many more and better reasons why they should have from five to ten. Women arrogate to themselves the freedom to say how many children they shall have and when they shall have them. One thing we know: the "best" stock is showing the smallest reproduction.

Propagation and its entailments may not be essential to the health of women, but they promote it enormously, and their absence engenders mental and emotional disequilibrium. There would be small call for specialists of my sort if men and women married early and successfully. Every diagnostician has "hunches." I have a hunch that the sex-coefficient of many of these writers is low.

The women who wrote the articles under discussion have all achieved a measure of success in varied careers. Yet they say little of their duty toward the race. Most of them mention men only as they have observed them in their youth, particularly in their fathers, and they maintain a deep silence about child-bearing. Nine of the group do not even mention it, still less do they imply that they have given it a thought. Two were so terrified at the idea that they decided never to procreate; one wanted children, though without marriage, and in the end had neither. One is a confirmed celibate and satisfied with it as she is with everything she has done, and one "lives in sin" and is childless. This alone is a terrifying discovery. If these women are so steeped in their desire for social freedom and economic rights that they disregard entirely their first prerogative, what will become of the race they claim to uphold? Despite the celibate's self-complacency, her life is incomplete. To pretend that she has handled the marriage problem by avoiding love in or out of marriage is fatuous.

One of the writers with a sense of humor has decided that her feminism and convictions about self-support are not powerful enough to destroy the happiness she feels at being supported by her husband. One preaches need of financial independence for women as a self-respecting basis for love and marriage (why love?) while another declares it has nothing to do with them: "It is the spirit of cooperation that counts and enables two people to make adjustments." A third has discovered that marriage is "the only profound human experience," and another consented to it after thirty-odd years of celibacy as the only way in which "one can give expression to love without interference."

I am disappointed that I find no discussion of the relation of pleasure to work. One admits that she hates work and sees no necessity for it even if it is needed to uphold feminist doctrines. To be sure, the five writers or journalists agree that they like the economic independence their work gives them, but they possess some of the sacred fire that makes for efficient work. The four teachers are engrossed with the ideal aspect of their careers, and the one social worker renounced it when she felt the discrepancy between her ideals and practise; she is the most ardent and militant feminist of the group.

Has station in life anything to do with feminism, or is it by sheer coincidence that, with one exception, these women were born to poverty? It would be interesting to have a series of articles on the same subject by women born to riches. If it would not affect their views on marriage and children, it might on feminism. The woman who, in her struggle for existence, hurts the wings of her ideals against hard walls erected by man is likely to overstress the necessity for independence of every kind.

Few of the writers, obviously, are under forty, and many of them are much older. Their efforts were made at a time when the struggle was real; now they take on the aspect of pioneer work. These women have "arrived" by their own means and their stories should be illuminating. They would have been so had the writers taken full advantage of their anonymity to reveal the soul in conflict between love and the principles and practice of feminism.

Were I seeking examples to illustrate that temperament and talent are inherited and not acquired, I could ask for no better ones than this series of articles furnishes. Nearly every one of the writers had at least one parent entitled to be called intellectual, with a desire for books and knowledge, and a determination that his or her offspring should have an education. It is interesting, too, that ten of these women had energetic, determined, dominating mothers, the kind that often shapes docile, dependent daughters and has sons with a flair for the easiest way.

On rereading these articles I fell into meditation. Which of these women should I have liked to companion?

There were two with whom I should have been willing to attempt it. One had strong, lusty desires and she wished more than anything else to have "swift feet that she might run after them." Another who interests me wrote the twelfth instalment. She seems to have neither ambition nor determination to administer the world, and she knows how to laugh and be joyous. She thinks the earth a lovely place to live and her only reason for being a feminist is dictated not by effect but by intellect. If her buoyant spirit has not made her over-affable I think she would be my first choice.

Turning to the corollary of this meditation, I wondered which of these women would be my last choice. Again it simmered down to two: The second and the fourth. The former had a childish sense of guilt. The grief and gloom of her parents was that they had brought her into the world, and she has a passionate desire to be no trouble to her husband. The fourth says that "no living person can give me the excitement I got at eight years old when my father took me on his knees and popularized the theories of Darwin for me." I should hesitate to enter as a contestant with father!